An unnamed narrator, podreaming, or already dead, or as good as, being an exile, or a condemned fool on a ship of fools, takes the opportunity of this voyage of sorts, to try and make sense of their life and mental state. Through a dizzying, meandering syntax, and farcical flourish, the adventure takes us through philosophical events with dogs, how to tell one's tale, plead one's case, how to walk through doors, lose one's limbs, if not one's mind, how to make a liveable self in the world, while puffing out smokes of language to fight off the existential crisis at play: "I am waiting for something to wait for." It might take a little while to adjust to this spinning language feast, adapted from bygone literary models, from Rabelais to Sterne, but once you're in, you will find yourself unable to put down the addictive, comical, and strangely urgent twists and turns of Seidenberg's latest proposition.
—Caroline Bergvall, author of *Drift*, *Alisoun Sings*, and *Meddle English*

In his captivating *Coda*, Steven Seidenberg combines philosophy, narrative, and poetry to grapple with the ontological basis of perceptual multiplicity, the universal posture of a subjectivity unanchored in substance. Readers of *Coda* encounter an "I" struggling against a sea of recollections, but neither in the mode of a heroic odyssey that sets its teleology on a mythic home, nor a mystical union with the One, guided by a leeward yearning for autobiographical shores. The sea is here a figure of travail and a motion that wrests the writer from stable "ground" to an epistemological cataract, a compulsive skirr towards being that is at once a glimmer of disclosure and a final obfuscation—"the last place, the final placement, and the spent world in tranquility and rancor," a dream we call place. *Coda* is ultimately a story of beginnings without origin, and endings that digress beyond all possible conclusion; in ecstatic derivation and surrender to this paradox at the center of all psychological and philosophical resolve, Seidenberg has created a genre-defying work that transfigures the pre-modern forms of fable, treatise, panegyric, and novel into something entirely new, a tragic/comic mashup that extends beyond description.
—Tarek Elhaik, Professor of Anthropology, University of California, Davis, author of *Aesthetics and Anthropology: Cogitations* and *The Incurable-Image: Curating Post-Mexican Film and Media Arts*

Also by Steven Seidenberg

Literature

Anon, Omnidawn Publishing, 2022

plain sight, Roof Books, 2020

Situ, Black Sun Lit, 2018

Null Set, Spooky Actions Books, 2015

Itch, RAW ArT Press, 2014

Photobooks

The Architecture of Silence: Abandoned Lives of the Italian South, Contrasto, 2023

Pipevalve: Berlin, Lodima, 2017

coda

© Copyright Steven Seidenberg, 2025. All rights reserved.

Cover art and design by Steven Seidenberg
Cover typeface: Bauhaus 93

Interior design by Laura Joakimson
Interior typeface: Garamond Premier Pro

Library of Congress Cataloging-in-Publication Data

Names: Seidenberg, Steven (Steven J.) author
Title: Coda / Steven Seidenberg.
Description: Oakland, California : Omnidawn Publishing, 2025. | Summary: "The nameless narrator of Steven Seidenberg's latest work, Coda, attempts to trace the origins of linguistic and perceptual differentiation—of experience through the cipher of the subject, broadly understood—by advancing the linguistic experiments of contemporary lyric and narrative forms, moving between extravagant prosody and obsessive disquisition to reconfigure the conceptual imperatives common to many throughlines in philosophy and theology. Continuing the focus on the structure of memory and the decadence of body he began in his book Anon, Seidenberg here describes the epistemological regress of desire, intention, knowledge, and discernment, coupling the language and concerns of authors as diverse as Spinoza, Kant, Hegel, and Wittgenstein with a raucous humor in the tradition of Rabelais, Beckett, Lispector, and Sterne"—Provided by publisher.

Identifiers: LCCN 2025010331 | ISBN 9781632431738 trade paperback
Subjects: LCGFT: Narrative poetry | Experimental poetry
Classification: LCC PS3619.E4193 C63 2025 | DDC 811/.6--dc23/eng/20250310
LC record available at https://lccn.loc.gov/2025010331

Published by Omnidawn Publishing, Oakland, California
www.omnidawn.com
10 9 8 7 6 5 4 3 2 1
ISBN: 978-1-63243-173-8

Steven Seidenberg

OMNIDAWN PUBLISHING
OAKLAND, CALIFORNIA
2025

I

Seeing we are at leisure, and that I may contuse your lungs with laughter no divinity will hear, I remind you I am nothing, I am no one, I am nowhere, a revenant innominate, and implore you call me anything your conscience and coincidence—your recognized resemblance—would alloy to my good nature, or unwittingly prefer. I am your humble witness…your *deponent* in this fracas, both eager to increase the spleen that draws your convalescence to its feral pique, its dreamless near, and to whirl another verticil of subterfuge and pretext, as the forthcoming embodiment of ideal interlocutors demands…

φ

It may appear imprudent to profane the middle margins of this withering excursus with such malign solicitude and affable defiance, a contraindication to the manifest emergence—the clarity of purpose—that led you to its doorstep, but that is not your business, any more than my concern; I seek no consolation in some impotent avowal or its ersatz diagnosis, fixed within this harmony of negligence and disrepair. If indeed it's understood I have begun at all, and that by nothing more than this apportioning of paragraphs into such a melodious rose of a form, so be it—each petal tolls a counterpoint unheard since first dislimned this vengeful parody of progress…

φ

Let us recall together, then, my life upon the main, my longing to evade the undiscovered throes of some fated ontogeny by plotting a surrender to the fleeing tide, the leeward gaze, and the subsequently ascertained mendacity of my disclosures, amidst the bleary slur of lo these many fickle thrusts and jaded parries. Indeed, the mere acceptance of my previous imposture—convening such reproof to its rhetorical avail—serves to guarantee this stipulated misadventure, without which my confession would never have acceded to the differential patter of its lyric gale...

φ

And though I know that some of you have firstly been informed of my foremost compendium of escapades and apothegms by this crude affidavit of its sanative effects, through said conjecture having been apprised of where the thrilling chronicle of its return to relevance broke off, I anticipate an interlude in my circumlocution is of so little import to your expected entrée into its remitting midst you won't give it a second thought. I surmise, that is to say, the concomitant consonance resulting from your bearing bored aboard the redirected transport of this rotted husk—this leaky float—allowing that our comity contrives a fixed reliance...a near interdependence of reciprocal directives in the dispatch of this codex of seductions and bereavements, from bottle set adrift athwart the echo of the waves, to anonymous receiver on some distant shoal...

φ

Alas, I fear the reciprocity of which I speak and for which I have spoken does not speak of the same humor for us both. My mistake was in accepting we had met at some disjuncture I have no way of knowing that you've ever deigned transgress, and yours is less mistake than the presumption of an absence, of your *not* having this pastiche of minutiae at the ready while we ready to embark; while we recall the launch of our generic embarkation, as if our last beginning can continue to invigorate the prospect of a first before all others, the dislocated *first* first that compels us to the measure of all precedents and paragons to follow...

φ

In all I fully recognize the wise and wily members of this coddled tribe no less inclined to sidestep such professions of false promises—promises made only *to retract*—but that will not dissuade me; you'll note my general practice of forsaking such advice in the achievement of communion—if not precisely commutation—and I'll do no different now in adhering to my path. A path, you will agree, that started somewhere...*began sometime*—so the telling of the telling will decidedly elapse. Your facile schemes, your fretful chidings...why must we pretend that we have braved this run together, that our times and ways of passing time move on a standard gauge of track? We come upon our commonweal by virtue of...*by virtue*, and it's only your good will and genteel custom that still bind us to this shared resolve, this common gap...

φ

Why not *take a stab*, that is, at recapitulation, and acknowledge our proclivities as *equal* and not *prior* to their final degradation into form—the measure of the conquest I would as much coerce across the plain of this transcendence, if not compel to practice through the sensor of the corpus, the scarified remainder of an unremembered scrum. I can't account for those of you who've come upon this apologue without prior exposure to its fundamental plan, but there are reasons for my having left off in that muddle of a masterpiece, alleged to be continued by the unheard and unchallenged implications of some recondite anon, as everything resultant only musters to necessity given your unwavering collusion...

φ

Reasons in the *plural*, this I won't deny—and perhaps none ranks as greater than the move towards a synopsis, a redaction of past influences; one brooks that what seemed pivotal at one point in our fellowship can flounder through the trauma of its trivialization, once sufficient time has passed for those who first encountered it to vacate, then rejoin. How plainly shall I put it? Do I merely carry on? What is it *to you* if I should blather and perseverate, or try to assess blame? You are my confidante, it's true, but penance and purgation are neither yours to grant nor mine to squander, and what I stand to reap from our familiarity is both more *and* less than any shout of tribute from the aisles can provide...

φ

In this one case, I feel I'm coming round to your position—or *assuming* it, I think it's better put; I'm taking on the affect of an outcast to my own collated predicates, a conflation of conditions that barters an alignment of incentives for a requisite resistance—an *inimical* preponderance—tantamount to proffering the cosmos in suspension, in partisan arrangement and correlative relief. I feel that I've been with you...that I've *taken on* your presence, and though I know your troubles will remain wholly your own, I anticipate the ouster of these turgid liabilities from the register of my affairs will ease your tideworn journey, crossing over...

φ

But before you raise your hackles at such august claims of service—or withdraw your loath compliance, your *coerced* assent—permit me to assure you that I understand the problem, an obstacle I feel an obligation to surmount; that already in this archive of contortions and dilemmas I've alluded to the tokens of another in the past—by method of a cursory remembrance of its details, and a similarly speculative allusion to its faults; another whose portrayal you may not know is extant, or existed before this one—so this litany of pilfered shards and random filiations in fulfillment of said vouchers only reads as problematic for the absence of substantive, as though a jointly held bequest...

φ

Still I know this rationale is no excuse to riddle my dear readers with complaints or commendations in which, as mere observers to the indignity of this inaugural conspectus, they hold little or no share. That the aforementioned chronicle of my distinct morphology has hardly met *your* notice in relinquishing this digital remainder to the scene must recognize that some of you have yet to cull our last chance at acquaintance from the transcripts and portfolios dispersed about the ambit of your cluttered close—your soiled pen—a deficit I'll try to fill before you lose your focus, intending to elude the accusations of obscurity that hound my tropes and standards no matter how I supplicate before the critic's judgment, or the tideway trends...

φ

Which is not to say I'll soon indulge my appetite for disruption, a denial that performs what it foretokens to deny...I don't want to *perplex*, that is, my dissolute admirers as they seize the opportunity to first perplex themselves, but patience here will demonstrate the force of my conjectures, freeing the circuitous delirium of confidence from undisclosed confinements of its *doxa*. In this sense I have taken on the role of explicator, in succession liege and vassal to my unsuspecting charge—thus you become apparent, thus you have appeared; the second, after all, will always chance at pleading singular, even after forcible enlistment to accord, and this is the compulsion I encourage you to satisfy, despite your desperation to surrender to the fold...

φ

And how might such a summary amount to an advancement? What course could it take, that it might keep this gentle rivulet from damming up with mud? Do you think that it's so easy to tell tales of tales while plundering some fetid heap of tailings for a mislaid revelation? To reform these paltry details into sacrificial code? I'll do my best to carry off this venery as predator, a rarity for one who's only ever served as prey, though you alone are able to accept my throttled resources, without in turn proclaiming me the quarry once again. You alone possess the clout to vacate my conviction, but first I spin a cautionary yarn you may unspool as oft you like; or disregard my detour as a ploy to win a chortle, but you do so as a danger to us both...

φ

There lived in Königsberg a cruel eccentric who would leave his house each afternoon with a block of marble balanced on his head, and stumbling upon an unsuspecting dog, would drop the stone straight down upon its tail; unduly vexed, the beast would run about in stunned confusion, chasing and fleeing at the same time. It happened that among the casualties of this prank was a dog whose owner—a milliner by profession—loved it very much. The block dropped on the dog's tail, the dog raised a fuss; the milliner saw the trespass, and defended the dog with a yardstick. With every thwack the milliner yelled: "My pointer? Didn't you see, you vicious fool, that my dog is a pointer?" repeating the word *pointer* many times. Battered and abashed, the abused abuser didn't go out for more than a month, but finally reverted to his clockwork traipse adorned with an even heavier chunk. Approaching dog after dog, he examined each one and proclaimed: "This one is a pointer, watch out!" So every dog, whether mastiff or lap dog, poodle or terrier, immediately became a pointer, and the block never dropped again…

φ

Turnings of the sort in any diegetic artifice, already nearly spent for its enfeebling prolixity and droll recriminations, are awkward enough; enough to be assured all those who've traced its path as witness— who've cruised this choppy runnel with such stamina and kismet— should likely go no further, for the blatant insufficiency of what has come before. Accepting, then, its relevance on first consideration—as though a first could ever first come now—I here forsake the prospect, I won't allow that it was so, aware I've done just that by the performative assertion of the contrary…

φ

Why, you may have asked, would such a drudge as this, occasionally of keen insight, not *without* sense of propriety, who had real *positions* to communicate, resolve to do so in a shape bordering so closely on the absurd? Might not such a one, in striving with characteristic vehemence to render some pelagic scene upon the canvas, and ever thwarted in those attempts, dash a sponge full of all colors against it, to find whether it might at least paint *foam*? Here, however, can the present editor, with a narcotic tranquility as of over-weariness falling into sleep, find another way to pass the time while searching sight of spout on the horizon...

φ

Well does this dissembler know, if previous testimony be worth anything at all, that to innumerable readers such intrigue will not yield a favorable consummation; and that the yearning cohort drawn to browse my rants and ravings will consider this divergence, during these crucial intervening years and paths and pages, an uneasy disturbance to their ways of thought and digestion—so they indicate as much with an explosive borborygmus and even spoken invective—through all of which, as with other mercies, ought they not to thank their shrewd proprietor for the pained release inspired by such folly? To one and all of you, O irritated readers, with outstretched arms and open heart, I bid a kind farewell...

φ

Have we not, in the course of mapping out our fractional eternity, traveled some length of our life's journey in sight of one another? Have we not endured together, though betimes in state of quarrel? It is my belief we shoulder similar burdens under similar restraints, and that these likenesses are spread to every common form of furlough and pursuit—to pratfalls and waterfalls, shore leaves and sabbatical leaves, spa resorts and last resorts; to seizures of assets and seizures of cortex, philosophic rigor and its corresponding mortice, flailing fits and flailing fists, jumps and jaunts and counterfeit attempts at melioration; to seawalls breaking with the rise, harbors conquered by the tides, forest hamlets melted by the forests as they burn; to flop sweats and bomb threats, bone breaks and jonesing shakes, scalpel cuts and needle ruts, excarnation, incarnation, and being born again...

φ

So, it seems, I have begun, begun to set the stage anew, as you have surely noticed, and should I have accomplished such a pageant of dissemblance by alleging the commencement I've continued since to warrant, I'd most certainly have ended prior to it. Every preface thus conveyed endeavors an impossible foreboding of persistence, but finding resolution in its retrospective limits, presumes to have begun before...before the recollection that there was a time before... must always have commenced as though in excess of its discharge into prospect—into *outset*—ensuring the retrenchment of what otherwise disorders its topology of predicate effects...

φ

Such pointing towards a pointing towards the primal passe-partout of some crude pointer seems to yet have pointed towards a nebulous beyond, a summary assemblage I claim fortitude to mention only as and by my longing to maintain an otherwise excruciating savor, the immedicable immediacy of every intermediate arousal towards an imminent resolve. Permit me, then, to sublimate this obstinate avowal for something like a general inclination to proceed, to finally *and for the last* repeat what I have formerly voiced only as a mantra, the vow of ready action sputtered underneath my breath...

φ

There is a purity in the silence, an ease of thought and motion I have seemingly embraced, but I disclaim the affect for your unruly tenancy, hoping you might someday come to apprehend the favor, or recognize the sacrifice I make by this abandon to the feint of *showing forth*; I think that after all I must be making a piece of cloth, not by virtue of repetition or intent, rather because I am sitting at a loom, and performing the motions I associate with its use. But I am no such weaver, of sails or schemes or portents. I work the carpet of causation with the delicacy of mangled stumps, beating heavy mitts upon the symmetry of its seemingly reticulate design. So the presentation of the pantomime to follow—that assembles this coherence as a doorway, and a frame—is all that differentiates the second from the plural—and the exigent apostrophe of some presumed precipitate from joining the dejecta of subsidiary modes...

φ

I'll venture what I must, that is, acknowledging that merely being *patterned* as an argument is no evidence of proof, but I assure you that the form of my compulsion to pursuit is more than spectacle—more than given to *distract*—and make this same admission in order to avoid attaching guilt to our inconsequence, as though the troth of agency could stand in for requite. I'll venture what I must, I say, and neither more nor less; thus my ragged theorems and their paroxysmal phrasings will prove exhortative in this one way—those who apprehend them will recognize their obsolescence, and move towards the dismissal of the same...

φ

In accordance with the crease of such propitious observation—and the incidental manifest to which it pertains—one supposes an imperium of knowable particulars held in shared proportion with one's purported cohort, by implicated reference to the judgment that esteems such given stimuli as *real*. Whereof one cannot speak, as of a diacritic orifice, thereof one must entreat a novel stratagem of signs; thus I have envisaged so much more that might have been, it's difficult to stop from listing all the indications of a world at once foretokened and impossibly delayed, disparate though they seem, but so I must, and so I will, for dread of having nothing left, and leaving nothing...

φ

I shiver as I wallow in the welter where I lie, mustering my mute and indiscriminate admirers, whose missing admonitions—an opulence of lost replies—embolden this expectancy, this lesson learned and proffered as position, then as portent, then as havoc, then as rule: Nothing is going to happen, nothing is happening to me. Nothing is going to happen that hasn't happened already, and anyone who'll ever think to conquer such arousal has been pardoned and defeated—by having thrown themselves upon the mercy of this vatic scam. Why then here does anyone step forth? Gleaners, such as you and I, are alone enjoined to make a survey of the wreckage, and fashion what remains into...

II

All this that I ask myself, all this quizzical abandon, emanates from no distaste for what remains impulsive or uncertain, as the unexpected vestige of a bygone ache, or the ancillary moorings of a wayward skiff; the voyage must go on, I say, undaunted by indifference, a rhetoric of pace and drift that can't be interdicted. The voyage must go on—who could have the strength to doubt it; and as in dispossession from the land resides the highest truth, indefinite as any godly spasm from the null, so better to vanish in the storm surge of that squall than to beat one's addled noggin on the cudgel of the shore—to flow again as water spilled, and gathered to the sea...

φ

Soon it will emerge that I have torn myself asunder that my diffident detractors might be spared the same in turn; so I launch this contravention of my previous departures as a warning and remembrance, not a dogma, or a vow—no adventure shall proceed without the relevance of these ignoble portents readied to the register of every anxious subaltern conceived to meet its view, no obscure relation shall be taken for the first dim coalescence of an emblem, or a parable, even as some turgid mope who comes upon the counterfeit may strive to rend the chrysalis of happenstance, to thereby gain a slot within some transcendental mold; may yet *assert* some hermeneutic cordon as a cipher, or an oracle...

φ

Does not the leery dramaturge but set an idle cleverness against the somber advent arc of every yarn unspooled, with the disparaging flourishes of the dilettante masked only by the furtive excesses of the academy? Certainly the difference—that I am not, that I have never been, an equal to my predicates or any fain description of them—is neither obvious nor clear, neither clear nor distinct, let alone both, and for this reason I oblige such a retelling by employing the same method of remembrance I have formerly reproved, guilty of the blundering delinquency most usually ascribed to the arrogance of a dull wit, by having here engaged in that ascription...

φ

And given just the right turn of phrase, I might agree with the sentiment that motivates this mooting interrogatory, to finally effect the sullen brodie I so long ago devised as but a bit of careless whimsy, and formulate an end to all these unabashed abasements. If I ever thought it could be, then perhaps...perhaps it would, and some still brighter star would here descend to take my place. But it is not my way, I pursue a different course, leading my indicters through the marvels of this quizzical intransigence with nothing but a silent suspiration for a nudge, knowing that the pause is a procession all its own, assuming pride of place before what will precede it...

φ

You'll note that though I've since allowed the ill-defined compulsions of the technique I've disparaged in the telling as means to do just that—to tell at all, that is to say, with such crude vigor and deceit—it's not my indiscretion that's allowed the inconsistency to stand, but my belief that the enactment of the fallacy upon itself will compel a more organic stripe of ease and comprehension in its presumptive proctor—its indifferent ward. I appreciate there's no account of disinterred receivers that can adequately recognize the forfeiture inherent in their spurning of some more established plan, providing this submission to a contrary disclosure does not attain commensurate accession to its perquisites—despite the seeming lethargy of hearing them divulged—but such appreciation ought not be mistaken for the sanction of its ouster, as I have been unknowingly made party to the fraud…

φ

There is reason to consider it, if only for a moment; should I take it as my task to indicate the specious leap of ratiocination to one who first commits it, and whose nature is characteristic—if only by that, if by that alone—of my nature equally, then what could more convincingly prevent the next indulgence of the dudgeon than the manifest deficiencies of the practice, the *reductio ad redundum* of this devious battology? Is it not a commonplace of competent polemic to unconceal the fallacy by measuring its fit against the raveling integument of truth, just as one is only able to discern the finest cloth by living for a time within the poorly loomed and finished…

φ

Every truth propounded must withstand this routine trial, born forever closer to its claimed corroboration by its falsification in principle, and the subsequent abeyance of its postural antithesis in having been shown counter *to itself*. Most significantly, my narration of previous and forthcoming adventures remains as far from allegory as any random shopping list, declaiming not the nothing of my motives and displacements by each instance of the insult so much as the indifference of all categorical exertions to the contrary. A god when I dream, a beggar when I undertake to apprehend the dreaming...

φ

Here and once again does the peremptory preferment of a subject...of *subjectivity* within every reductive reminiscence seat the interregnum of a first, if only by determining its incidental absence, the final and unfaltering disseverance of the infinite from all iterative regress in its series. Is there some novel precept thereby fashioned as permitted, that should it have been noticed first would curb this exegesis from its boorish prodigality? The science of the foremost must propose a past epitome of the next purposive primacy, positioning the first as that—as tendered and transfigured by the sequence its positioning completes—where the same thought thought as some elucidation of the rank could never of its essence keep its place within that consecution...

φ

One can be assured, that is, that first recalled—and first recalled as first—was not the first there was, could not have ever been, for as the steady cadence of what always was to follow is conceived by the propinquity that holds that arbitrary designate in place—fixed within its phalanx by its ordinal constitution as a placement—the tendrils of mimesis spread in and through those varied harbingers and their proximate paresis just as long before as after. Every first is first conceived a secondary act of indication by the supplemental indices encompassing its orbit of discernible effects; whence that same discerning subject present prior to discernment of its requisite adornments is constructed as a substrate of all that it foretokens as precipitate...

φ

The disparity rests precisely in this implicit mandate—to apprehend awareness of the apprehending subject as the first sense, to presume that same acclivity as given, and through said premise understand the sense of any subject thus subjected as the first that ever was or could have been. By having *presupposed*, that is, the sense of sensing prior to revealing such a focus of peripheral reception as the first—as first *from* the first, whatever first in series will succeed it—one accelerates a further supplication to its margin…to the sense of *passing through* that makes for its delineation, and forthwith differentiates the sense of the sense of the subject, the sense of the subject, the subject, sanctioned as the ever-present figure of the primacy of sense, from the sense of such a subject before that understanding can be understood as having always already arisen—as the limit *of a process*, so a *coming to* completion that is never at its margin, never managed as a terminus…

φ

In a freer style, a mélange of quirks and contingencies, such method of investigation invests itself in ordinary life—in a conversation, say, or in the kind of chronicle that satisfies curiosity more than it results in knowledge—just as a preface marks a mode of recapitulation, rather than a manner of commencement. And though my wary readership may squirm at the acceptance of a proof where none's been granted—a propensity determined as much by a passivity of intellect as its prospective missive—knowing the difference always implies…*entails* the telling of it, and telling equally its knowing, allowing each must of its own inflexible initiative posit—what, I say, but one, a subject, the sense of a subject, the sense of the sense of a subject, and so on…

φ

What else could be first, that I should disregard the gift of this most critical of canons? If the sense that *I am I* accompanies all nervous stimulation of my focal apparatus—as the centrifugal filter of the impetus it names—then what other could precede it...could be supposed without it—what other that would not occur below... beneath...*outside* the plenum peel of that sequestered perlustration? I perceive many disparities of posture and position, many moments in succession, many distances and forms, and each to each to sense each one requires some prevailing I to sense them; I fix the connate paradigm of my inferred distinction by being fixed within it—by signifying everything that's never been the subject of such comprehensive inference, what manifests the dissonance of all that lies extrinsic as a shadow, or a screen...

φ

The only first that could have been before the first I sensed I sensed— before the sense that *I'm* the one who senses—is that of the divergence of the substance of sense—the *in* of that I am *as* sense—from all that differentiates the always ever *out*. I am only posed as extant—am only *am*, in whole or part—as affect of the substance that I would be if I weren't, even as the generalized particulars of such construed persistence still elude the supplication that allows the sensing subject to observe its own presentiment, its coming into being as itself; I would not be this *what-I-am* or *as-I-was* if ever I'd been able to achieve the pretermission of the *what* and *as* I'm not...

φ

It may be an uncomfortable conclusion, if such a call to worship can be thought of as conclusory at all, but so must the intrepid climber follow the deft footfalls blazed by your most modest servant of a pathfinder, pedigreed by filth and wail against the vain allurements of a slumber in the clouds. I would have nothing had I not this principle alone; I would have nothing, so it seems, were I not nothing, and I would not be nothing were I not also something in my way—a supplement only as dangerous as it is definitive, the *causa sui* that precedes all recollections of such unrequited precedence...

φ

I lug this languid *nous* about the sterile and the quick, forcing every portent of life-giving breath to atrophy within the wizened pith on which my glutted hollow has been shimmied. So I leap back by leaping forward, just as secure in my reasoning and my wit, both inadequate to the project at hand—whatever may be fashioned by the figure of a competence as poorly defined as its approach is distant—and neither having met the standard of fulfillment that is my seeming purpose. Not everyone crawls out of this world satisfied—or into it, for that matter, or into it...

φ

If it's tacitly assumed all this should end by never ending, then it's well within my purview to surrender, and proceed; I have done as much already—refused the boon and stipend such an inkling of the infinite inherently bestows—and here I take the impulse for another aberration, exchanging the pleasures of a passive resolution for a fealty to the fitness of its inferential code. Every primacy presents the unforgiving physics of a center, the one continent that—forever in the middle—inscribes all that surrounds it by investing its exterior with the portents of its predicates and stains; so my land is all meridian, were it not, I had not fled my clime, through sickled voids and muddied troughs, nor would I be, in spite of insults never to be forgot, indentured to this reckoning, its every blatant amity or hidden sop, and finally enraptured by the silhouette and witting watch—of thee…

φ

Engendered as the prisoner of such a heedless drift, the axial remainder of the bounding sense of sense, I know there's nothing garrisoned within this porous bilge not also arrayed topside, nothing *in* or *out* but for that percolating capsule of superfluous attentions, the bowered *locus solus* of the reliquary sward. How else could one sense, but to the point of an utter incapacity of distractions, faced with this archetypal inculcation of the form of forms? One flounders in the sludge of one's adjacent putrefaction, and peering through the shadow of one's semblance on the palisade, turns to find the source of light that paints that furtive umbrage fixed within the head—inside the shadow—hence from nowhere in particular, the orbital umbilicus of an image reproduced by the tracing of its outline in, its inline out, and pushing down…

φ

It makes perfect sense, it makes sense perfect; it consolidates so seamlessly…so *cohesively*, I can't find a way to claim I didn't claim it from the first—from the *first* first, even—as though I longed to feign a longing otherwise. I know that I did, that I wouldn't have arrived here had I taken up another course or understood the one thus took by any other analogue of bearing or concernment. The retrospective telos thus effected by such labor, the issue of each dolorous remainder I consort, acts alone to frame an ineluctable fixation, and by such intimation of compelled design maintains the leveled reservoir of judgment that I trudge through, punch-drunk and without escape, transfixed by that hypostasis of flatness…

φ

For just as all sense is composed of the equivocal duration that transcends it while one's in it, no mere happenstance confines the sense that *was* within the sense that *is*—that makes it there at all, that is, as though there were no other sense before it; no sense makes sense before sense, there is neither there nor sense before sense, but something else, something other than sense—*non-sense*—is all that occupies the place of that insuperable precedence. That every sense must make sense in and of itself is in itself what makes sense *of-itself* and of the *in-itself* the same, for so the sense of sense construes sense sensible as such—*endeavors* its apparent sensibility, that is—and must preside therein as though the infinite declension of that preceding portion…

φ

All to bring about the next conclusory abatement, that the substance of sense, inclusive of the sense of the substance of sense, can only find its operative center in the project…the *event* of subjectivity, always fixed within the ancillary it contrives, and equally the obverse implication—that the sense of the substance of sense can never discharge, neither express, the tableau of its inception, but attends to its effulgence only after understanding the subsistence of that sensing as the subject of a predicate expectancy, an oculus adrift above the amplitude it constitutes by nothing more than gazing, though even here, even here…

φ

Even here there is no landscape, neither index to dragoon the breach of everything that *makes the case* from integrated viscera to image on the canvas. The same resistance even here administers its imbrued simulacrum as a fantasy of equipoise—a hesitating stasis—accepting I could never charge another with a purpose any greater than the dissonance that demarcates my own defrauding animus—and I do not do so, no, I would not trust some alter with such mutable fidelities—or such keen infidelities abjured. Even I, that is to say—provisioned against service to all clarity of consequence, the mistaking of veracity for *seeing through*—cannot imagine lying in my own limpid embrace, nor that of any other I've encountered on my path, and yet there are so many who repose within the clutches of a lustrous and simulated vigor, only carried to accord in affectation of a boundless self-denial, as though responding to another with such ardor is to equally depreciate one's own inbearing fortitude—one's putative *disposal*—and take it for a given incapacity...

φ

Never would I spurn a hatred mercifully applied, and the pall of nauseated glances sure to meet my own perfervid stride across the lowland lean of delta settles as the impact of my foul approach received, taking some more pleasant hue with every gape-mouthed inquiry to follow. I am neither better nor different...or I am both better *and* different for having come to the conclusion that I'm neither, the deviance of my own self-abnegation from the premise that initiates its next destructive turn, the one the source of love alone, the other its advancing spawn—both prospect and concealment of an augured execution...

φ

But what can I have ever gleaned of such consideration, given the comportment of this imprecated muse? Admitting I have known neither fidelity nor fondness—that I've never felt obliged to dote as donor or recipient—how can I descant about that dissipating warble, or likewise the facsimile that binds its outward mews? What consent distinguishes the trust evinced by so much winging poesy from casting the voluptuary source of its intents as the prediction of a forthcoming momentum? Or equally a faith in one's own inherent temperament, that the condensation of conviction might thicken into personhood, as a stock left on the flame too long, a heave upreared to meet the army hindered by the berm...

φ

The sense one is *is* referenced to the lineal distension of the sense of sensing sensing, requiring the substance of sense—of the sense I am in substance only, the substance only in the sense—be altogether fungible with respect to the commerce of sufficient reason, just as the iteration of every ductile order holds some ancillary posture as its principal necessity, each within its given contiguity and frame. Knowing this in just this way, and I must, I must, there is no use denying now, no use harping on the same old thing, and so easy to say what I fought so long to keep hidden, and which amounts in the end to telling in the way I want to tell, with affable opprobrium and tender disregard—the telling of the advent of the telling of the tale, whether through some latent prosody or regulative codicil, by the telling of the advent of the tail that telling tells...

φ

Knowing what I know I know and what I know I don't—the mutability of character imposed against the germinal impairment of its use—how perorate with confidence in signs and incantations, or avoid such obtuse formulae, for it to make a difference either way? How could one trust one's judgment, when that judgment must prefer a presence fixed beyond its object—an *entity* defined by the transcendence of the outside that remains its verge and limit, as a tacit brink? It is as every is, is all, it must be every only as it is, the idle play of sense and of the senses always spoken with a universal voice, and the sense of sense—the thinking of the sense and the sense of the thinking of the sense—constructed as the referent recalled by its prepotency in order to be...to have *ever* been the object of one's broadly misconstrued perambulations...

φ

What could it mean to claim a faith in all that is case—to say I trust what is *is*, after I've accepted my rendition of its limits? How derive it otherwise, when even my most devious of planned dissimulations—the consistently revealed mistake—is, as the sense it is, a sense had...a sense *I have*, and so presents a world in which such contrary excrescence is emergent, as if to prove that what one wants is only what is pleasing by appeal to the self-evidence of an assertion equal in its weight, that the pleasant is what designates the nature of one's wants...

φ

I trust the interior sufficiency of the nominative, a credence that precedes...that *names* the act of naming in its breakneck skirr; how understand the thingness of the thing—and the labor of discernment that indicates its *difference*—as not the thing it is, but something else... something that it only predisposes *towards*? Every substance furnished with such ponderable predicates implies a sameness in itself, to itself, even should that credible coincidence construe some deposition of distinctions still precluded from the previous it will...it was...it ever *might* have been. It means little, I say again, to say I trust what I sense or that I sense; what could I trust instead...could I *conceive* of trusting otherwise, would that it were I to trust at all...

φ

The sense that manifests the difference is already a remembrance of the same, and the thought of it...the thought of it is nothing less than the sense of the thought of it, equally no more. Do I not expect the impulse to uprear the gathered precincts of my withers will result in such a prepossessing charge? Even the paralysis that plagues some given portion postulates a confidence that such habituation will reveal the numbed appendage is no longer poised to launch its prescient transit to the world, as a formal exaltation or a camouflage of ballast, to be doffed at the evening's toilette...

φ

And rousing once again from the same unwitting torpor—feeling even then the stricken limb where once it strained—I'm assured the slack addendum has assumed a new guise beneath the bland and suffocating tarp of the sense of sense. So too the beguiling irruption...the phantom *sensitivity* of the nerve since deadened to all corollary circumstance is never the sense of something that it *isn't*—must always be the sense of *something*—if but the culmination of that dangling reticulate, trailing without function at the knee or wrist or elbow, at the turn of dimpled joint or the necrosis of the coccyx...

φ

The *truth* of sense—the self-identical horizon of its ever-present incidence—adduces an unquestionable purchase; that one senses a tail, say, or any other promontory tentacle, is all that yet confers the problematic of this specious predication. It is only ever judgment—the deferral of sense by the sense of sense—that refines one's indecision through the process of reproof; the sense itself cannot be wrong, it merely is, and that without the least qualification. Even the deception engineered to dupe the simpleton does not contain within it the pursuit of that result, which comes at the *expense* of the suspension of one's faith in the consistency of credence, or dispelled belief…

φ

The sense of sense is just as much an act of sensible receipt as the sense itself, and so adheres to the invariable attributes of any sense discerned, by virtue of one's sensing it as such; the sense that one is *thinking*—that some inquisitive encumbrance of intellect cowers round and shuttles through the centering of sense—cannot be false but for the judgment that reveals the nature, so the meaning, of this the sense or thought as sense or…I might soon come to think I was not thinking *that*—I thought I was, but I was not—as readily as realizing I was not sensing what had once appeared to open up before me as a gloss—I thought I had a limb there, I used to have a limb there, but now, it seems, I don't…

φ

In either case—which is to say, in any case at all—the substance of the sense *I* sense is indisputable; I sensed something, I thought something, and then thought something other that on further iteration proved a counter to the first I thought or thought I thought or sensed I thought or thought I sensed or thought I sensed I thought or thought I thought I sensed or sensed I thought I thought or sensed I thought I sensed—a collation of corrections that discloses each a regress incommensurate with the previous...with the sense of the previous sense, and the previous sense of the previous sense, distinguishing the always only former from what I then declare...what is then *revealed* the actuality of the sense—the *content* of the sense—a judgment always equal to the base accumulation of all present sense thought otherwise as subsequently previous or previously next...

φ

The sense now past is presently received as other than it was when it was present; is not, that is, *defined* as an inviolable presentiment, but rather as the juncture of each vagabond remembrance, the malleable substance of the sense of sense assembled, and the axis of the sensor thus implicitly secured. The sense of sense interrogates the inside outside inside of the verge whose transitivity the sense itself contrives—each image of the sense recalls another sense entirely, the sense of sense the same, as the surfeit of impressions builds unto a requiem for every sensing subject thus collated to its final and efficient cause, which is to say—its *declination*...

φ

The substance of the sense of sense diverges from the substance of sense in that it is not present in the sense of...of any *it* perceived as extant and extended, even as the sense of substance is intrinsic to each instance of the span to which it seemingly refers, figured through all other incidental means and random measures. Thus by the inducement of this dubious reflection—by every adventitious, if contiguous, correction—each previous comportment of the sense of sense is signified as just and only part, while its fitful fragmentation suggests a supervenient coherence fixed within that scattered quantum, that congruity revoked...

φ

Why allege that any one constitutive discernment—or incitement towards some guaranteed conscription to belief—will continue only as it's been, regardless of the end that binds its novel sanction, or discommodes all lateral attempts? Can it be I am the victim, as you are given witness, of a genuine preoccupation—of a *need to know*, as one might say, and a duty to descant? Perhaps it's time I paid at least a *little* attention to my predicament, such as it may yet appear to those most fully capable of fending off the glamor of its integrated auspices and correlated acts...

φ

It will happen someday, one way or another, of this there is no question, deduced by the excrescence of these axioms and pages—these dreams and discontents—and made nearly as manifest through subsequent endeavors to diminish such productive length by feats of condensation, conceived and consecrated as anterior to substance, or posterior to intent. I nonetheless take note that some detractors of the practice assign such predilections to corrupt imagination, to an inner churn of anger or lust, ambition or contempt, which frequently replaces motive in their kind, and which is always on the verge of the elision of all that is right and true in the name of some inchoate cordon of coherence, deluding both with spectacle and fateful supposition, in variously mercurial passions and affections, and especially in fear of losing clarity of result...

φ

So the querulous concernment that initiates our progress from such facile hesitation to neglected masterwork: what will not a fearful mind conceive in the dark? What bugbears and devils, what iniquity and rot? And I would furthermore demand, in performance of respondent to this stimulating grouse: what needs all this before it's clear that such offense be given? If it be, I'll deny all, avoid all, renounce all I have said, and with as much facility excuse my failing affects, as others can as readily accuse me of a similar abuse. I presume of your good favor and acceptance for as long as you stay with me, and with such hope and confidence thereof, I will proceed...

III

To move with ease through open doors, they must have solid frames—a privilege I'm denied for having no means to indemnify this gramarye against the flux of wraiths and simulations, though if I could...*even* if I could it would not be enough to steady my domain within its system. This manifold of vestiges must always have been *come upon*...can never be devised by those who see it as beyond their wont to have pursued some nether sense distinctly stationed; no similar impediment can function as an index for the gambol of imperatives revealed by my precautions, or as evidence in support of the same sequence in reverse...

$$\varphi$$

Every sense affirms its pith both in and through the affect of its disparate anamnesis, compelling one to integrate the fungible largess of its remembrance as inscrutable concrescence, each amalgamation now discerned as indistinct from what that novelty now seems...now *is*—inextricably sublated to its advent. One fields the contiguity of sense as an awareness—the composition of its principle solicitude and setting—by recalling its relational exigency as perquisite, ascertained as other by the sense there that it is, that it was there as it will, that it will be as it was, filtered through the schist of every stratum of discernment...

φ

I cannot be correct in my appraisal of a fundament curtailed by this most monstrous of severalizing forms, nor can I treat of judgment in relation to that dissonance of attribute and cause; my sense can only flounder in the spate of recollections that indicates the term of its construal...its *insistence*, even as I recognize it only as it's *been*—always only as it's been *as such*. I occupy this vivified cadaver as an ersatz diving bell, salvaged from the mass of its imprisoning milieu by the discernment of the tentative intendments that gainsay its coherence, the organizing amplitude that grows between the inside and the out...

φ

But does one not still sense one's hidebound haunch with the facility that binds all other predicates to their variously circumscribed dependents—circumscribed by being the conveyance of all seeming circumscription? Must one always sense sense wrongly, the residue of some concealed synecdoche, there but to function as an exoteric goad? The sense of the body is determined as restrained by the attention of its importuning subject—its genitive, its *source*—successively composed in sense, through sense, as the intractable proscription of that polestar in its vessel, to last betray the sense of sense assembled, as endured...

φ

One might expect such vague resolve would authorize some novel probe to shroud the present problem, pushing it from focus while it moderates the view—if only it were so. If only I could presently move on...could *turn the page* on this palaver of a portion then that's what I would do, what I surely would have done, as therewith might the sense of sense—of the I that thereby senses—emerge as the catalyst of a requisite display, as the sense from which that trifling abstraction has apparently—always *formerly*—settled in its prison, and achieved its present term. I lie as I, I am not I, I tell I that I tell the difference I evince in some way that's distinct from what it is I think I am, or think I've been...

φ

Might one come to understand the sense of thought itself—the thought of thought *as sense*, that is—as but another phantom forced upon one's bounded bearing, the sensing as though present of what one no less knows is missing...is *transmissive*, in the bargain, towards an unknown addressee? Or the spectacle of each one's own progression into molder turn that scrutiny against itself, upon itself, so that the judgment...the *recollection* of the sense of the judgment, the judgment of the sense of the judgment—of the sense of *having judged*—would seem to be the groundwork of the sensate integration that invigorates the bearing of one's faculties...

φ

To extricate one token...one aspect...one *instance* of the sense of sense from any other equal in its stature or its form, one does by that same telling certify the falsity of the told, as it must be...*have always been* some other than it was or seemed it was, composed by the sense... the judgment...the *recollection* of its own inviolable parity, as though that same percipience could justify one's seeming independence from the scene. To have it means it is not had, or better still, it's been had falsely; to have it it cannot be had, and if it's had it's been had wrongly, never what it is for the surrendering of what it must appear to that first residue of status and resistance—of consciousness innate to every world in which it's understood as extant and extended, fettered as discerned. Which is not to claim the purview of some limpid universal more successful at discouraging the ragged permutations of this spiraling infinitive from *splitting*, as it were, without end; to implicate another singularity within oneself—a self that is at once interior and beyond—this seemingly objective authenticity must be presumed divergent from the sense that is its referent, composing the horizon of all patent sensibility as sense, by sense, *through* sense and its synthesis of fragmentary correlates…

φ

Levied to ignore the distal commonplace of imagery refracted through this scintillating dance of lights and baubles, one realizes that even the most convoluted roster of relations finds its cogency in nothing more imperative than such insipid doggerel, my métier and craft. If I have no other purpose—or have achieved no other ends—at least this supple cadence grounds the telling of the difference between the sense and the sense of the sense and the sense of the sense of the sense that first inspirited the impasse. That's what they want, after all, a simple allegory—a fairy tale would do just fine—as long as every detail guides a leitmotif in excess of its euphony and scansion, something grander for the sincerity of its varying objectives, more imperious for the proposed ubiquity of its drive; such a figural assemblage disabuses every arbitrary mantel of its character and standing, seeing not—as if it were to see—the deference of each difference to some inferred adjacency, never quite complete for every next that tarries where it ends and will begin again…

φ

One might look charitably upon these purveyors of a cultural nostalgia, pining away with a glint in the eye and a drink on the table, and accept the hubris of their telling entertainments for the sake of entertainment alone, but this is of scant value. Least of all is it my purpose to regale with apologia; I am no parishioner, and neither have I sought the hallowed blush of redress or lustration. Of more profound significance to my crude exegesis is that I am as I would be, the inadvertent object of the guile I proscribe—a substitute presentiment of every next and newly inescapable decedent...

φ

I wear the fluid soutane of this frayed metempsychosis as though it were a rash spread over some part since excised, a quondam itch I'm still compelled to scratch for the insuperable memory of its tingle. It is an analogue of some interest, though not enough to thwart the forward thrust of this advancing unconcealment, a feckless refutation of the substance of the subject that refutes. What matters is that first is only singularly primary if some other is coeval with the corpus of its consummate subtractions—to promise both the telling of an inferential chronicle, and the imprint of the subject whose persistence is alone devised of those same compositions told. There I was, I was myself, and yet I only know that I was there, that *there* and *I* were not the fiat of some retrospective phantom—the compensated dream of still another *lusus naturae*, wringing sodden tendons for the liquor of a prosody left otherwise unsung—by the persistence of the syndicate I occupy as sole and simple heritor of unrelated terms, without which I would not have had a sense of continuity thereafter...

φ

I still recall the stage on which I fell for the first time, playing to the favor of an aggregated absence, the guileless resistance of untrammeled ground, and peering through the halo of the arc lamp as it bloomed, my confines soon presented as not merely unfamiliar, but never before seen, a seldom-suffered accident in the sojourn from the annex to the backdrop, from the backdrop to the center cue; it's more accurate to suggest—so I thought it then just as I tell it now—that I had never thought myself intrinsic to that superficial fray, had never gazed upon that realm with any diligence at all, or if I had so gazed the sense was subsequently lost to some disjunctive reverie I also can't bring presently to focus or to mind...

φ

I remember climbing from that fleet prostration, there for the first conceiving of myself as I have subsequently been, noting with astonishment the ill-proportioned sepulcher into which I had arisen without mission or abandon, aware that should I then forgo attention to its amplitudes I'd never have the chance to know the place or time again. It might not be so great a loss, but I did not know that then, and so began a tally of those disparate appointments at my access, deciding what to bring along and what to leave behind on my first sally forth from that derangement; *determined*, I should say, to never want for something once in my possession but abandoned in a fit of unremarkable haste...

φ

There beneath the boards might lie some estimable bounty, and finding it I might be spared the need to scrounge but one more day's subsistence from the grime; I might find myself the heir to a pillaging of goods unwritten or recounted by the pasteurized histories that are all the rage, that are ever all the rage, acknowledging that any broadly credible mimesis—credible by being thus accredited, that is—must limn the gathered whimsies and droll acculturations from which that telling telling has ascended to be told. And should one stake the telling of the history of the telling of the history against that jumbled rationale of levers and controls, one must accept one has arrived at such conclusory abatements by the telling of a history itself absolved of all originary countenance, regardless of—and always disregarding—the succoring reproof that marks each next arising outside as extrinsic—as fixed beyond the pale of any thinkable repose…

φ

I recall it all just as it seemed, as if it ever were, though the recollection differs from what I've said already of that inherent scrutiny, the first that no way could have been…that could not have been first, for I recall it now as I alone, alone as I, and never through the lens of some projection of indifference, thrown upon another disparate centering of sense. There I felt myself exempt from all the adjutant conceits of that first cleaving indiscretion, as any empty gathering of presence for a cause, in which the exposition of my character and fitness had discomposed the harmony of what I dreamed the cover of an erstwhile nonpareil, a split from every previous extrusion of the genome…

φ

It's not as though I now recall that *what-I-was* as some distinctly other than the I who recollects it, for there I was as I am now, but only for the sense I have…the sense I had before of having been before do I suppose some reprobate identity, distant and receding, shuddering between the fore and aft that I remain—the singular intransigence of this that yields precipitate, as much the forging temper of a universal scansion as the distillate abduction of the subject firstly first as first of all. So conceived a refugee from providence or epoch, from any fateful reckoning through probity or aspect, I must presume I was before I knew of having been—before I had persisted as the stimulus my memory of such inceptive stimulation visits—for the recollection here surveyed with scrupulous disregard…

φ

I know I must have been before, before that then I was another I that after I was not. Just how long I've held to the position, immersed within the aggregate persistence of the role…I'm certain that I've known it from the first, for clinging to that tenancy as though it were the predicate periphery of awareness, a schema I've extracted from the latent superficies employed to importune these cogitations, whether driven to the pastureland of dissolute sufficiency I wander as a grazing lamb, or to another rube who can be similarly consoled. There before I was was I as yet another, for the nearly inescapable privation of all sense of having been…of having been before the foremost recollection of my having been before my having been…

φ

Is not the lolling neonate excited by *some* stimulus—whether irritant or lubricant, anodyne or jab—perhaps without the subtlety of more thorough perusal, but still and all a consciousness distinguished by that species of precognitive remove? And as that shrill concupiscence grows past its ill-formed latency into speech and all the mechanisms, physiological and otherwise, of speechifying ruse, it will always fail to recollect a sense of having been before its entrance into such denotative harborage, its cohesion with that primacy constructed as a miscellany lavished from the outside—as a gift unwrapped by the clumsiness of the giver, a prerogative to presence set beyond one's claim to consonance, thus to the *self*-possession of the corpus it encodes…

φ

Restricted to that register of novel sensitivity one can't conceive one ever *wasn't*, that one could have ever *not* been, the first vulgate ascension of the historical subject, abandoned to the acumen one reaches but a few short turnings of the seasons hence; one must assume a selfdom differentially persistent, even when the memory of each to whom the portent of such personhood applies does not support the view, but accepting the importance of some postulate or other doesn't constitute a reason for its extenuation, granted in advance of any cogent counterclaim…

φ

Any survey of the passage through minority so described will find it equally compelling to contrive such an inscrutable arrival by appealing to some dizzying assemblage of the kind, the *in-itself* that *of-itself* becomes another *for-itself*, fixed by the assignment of its own unpurposed eschaton. I am always only that I am, the lone impassive practicum arrayed upon the shuttle of the labile sense of sense, but my carcass laid to rot beneath the waves presents another fix entirely; it is not I, it can't be I, nor can it be considered as the substance of my singular cupidity…

φ

There must always be a back before the back, before the waxen hasp of any rigorous observance, whether fettered to its postulates or falling from its perch, requiring the bypass of a regress as baffling as it is inescapable; there must remain a first before the first conceived was ever first conceived as that—as for or as the first, that is—a first presumed before the rule of any first presumed, if one is to evade the repetition of that series, accepting that this postulate of primacy can only be thought adequate if it's also incomplete. One might find a certain confidence in answer to the paradox; I could rest within this gyre of reversals just as readily as break out again a step or two ahead of the morass, lying in repose to dissipate the entropy that churns the tidal vortex where the vessel sank...

φ

The exile is the instrument that sanctions the interior sufficiency of the fold; thus I venture a portrayal of the most distinguished turpitude—the zenith of all reasoned intellection and repose—to understand the range of its enclosure...its *declension*, ensuring that my sophistry abides within its staging, a performance thereby rendered as both practiced and controlled. I'll theorize in this instance I can span the void between us with the simplest of gestures, the merest of digressions as declamatory goad, and wager this exuberance to circumvent the tortures of a geometric standard, an exposé still struggling to inculcate before it can unravel, while mapping out a shortcut to a terminal repose...

φ

I'll make myself a dream, I'll make myself a memory, nothing but this voice and this silence, this circuit and collapse; every outcast from the fuselage is but part of the same portion, the amalgam of minutiae that bulk its bloated subterfuge considered as the threshold of a differential standard, in lieu of some revocable directive to attack. From the unexceptionable order prevalent in the granting of this clemency, I ask—what's the harm in moving on *before* one has the chance to clear the scene with caterwaul and incantation, pressed to serve the schema that uplifts one's parent domicile from its respite in the grave, or quickens it *with a push*...

IV

I ask you for your patience, your forgiveness and forbearance—it's how all this comes right in the end, how everything finds stillness and foundation, moves from difference to resemblance; it's thanks to vision that the darkness overtakes us, to the clamor of debasement that we settle in the quiet; thanks to the sun that burns that the sun burns no more, that time ends its ravening of our precincts and disclosures and suffering completes its chain in quietus, in lull and calm; we have nothing to do to do nothing, nothing to wait for to wait for nothing, there's no help in it, no help for it, nothing to help it, we will end where we belong, belong where we are, go back to where we started, and only then…

φ

So I stumble headlong into such considerations, as those I may be forced to set my mind to comprehend, perhaps to pardon, perhaps to sanction, perhaps only to witness, yet one warning let me give to those of my present or my future readers who are suffering such lethal or impetuous blight—that they read not the symptoms or prognostications in the ascendence of this tract as applicable to their person, trouble, or hurt, and in conclusion get more harm than good. I advise them therefore to peruse with caution, and brush or stand aside when the sentiment suggests. If through weakness, folly, passion, ornament, or ignorance I have said amiss, let it be forgiven and forgotten; I acknowledge that a dull blade is more likely to incise the one who holds it than a sharpened wit, for the absence of precision in its wielding…

φ

To put a cap on it, I am only as I am composed by telling…as the telling I've composed by telling…whatever path that indolent prolixity may take—whatever tale my tolling through this heap of tailings tells. It amounts to little more than the assertion—proffered as self-evident, though perhaps without just cause—that as the measure of the *reading*—forsooth as that alone—I've done just as I will, a doing that transcends the indiscretions of the neophyte by harboring this bleary pentimento of abstractions. How such indiscretion should be understood companionable—let alone *companioned*—despite being committed to a certain culmination in a capsize of the keel, is a question neither you nor I can answer without correlated effort—without affecting our *true* measure of the quandary, face to face…

φ

Fortunately, it's all a dream. For here there is no face, nor anything resembling one, nothing to reflect the joy of living or the fear of its rebuke. Imagine you've encountered something else, some simple thing, a box, a wooden chest, to interrupt your sightline for an instant. You find on its exterior evidence of grandeur, but also decadence; painted on the outside with lewd and naive figures, such as sleeping satyrs, bridled priests, demons herding human sheep into the devil's furnace; such as drunken harpies, saddled goats, choruses of lycanthropes, angels baiting saints to prove they're worthy of the firmament; all this you can envisage and other playful scenes to provoke you unto laughter or amusement, or for those more thoroughly indentured to the sovereignty of scruples, to repulse...

φ

Bear with me, then, while I expose my ludicrous exterior, such that if you laid your eyes upon me you would construe my jumble of an aspect as a masquerade—with the gaze of a child, and countenance of a fool; in carriage awkward, wanton in apparel, in fortune poor, unhappy in demeanor, unfit for all stations, always laughing at the wrong moment and crying when the crowd is chuffed with mirth, merrily skulking in the shadows and the margins, relishing the hurt that's harrowed every last decampment from the safety of my hovel, with continual taunts and jeers and betimes more violent blows, the better by those means to conceal my divine knowledge...

φ

Now, opening this box you have been assessed a heavenly and unsurpassed intoxication from its vapors—the waft of an unmitigated understanding, of universal virtue and matchless erudition, breathing the ambrosial fumes of inestimable foresight, of infallible certitude and ingenious disregard for all with which the many do so watch, run, swim, kiss, eat, fight, sink, shit, sleep, drink, wake, linger, toil, and generally disturb themselves. And put the case, that in the literal sense you meet with purposes sufficiently urgent and consequently correspondent to their inscriptions, yet you must not stop there, neither from temptation nor disdain, but endeavor to interpret in a sublime sense, a sense which possibly you intended to have spoken only in the secret courage of your heart...

φ

If you've ever witnessed how a dog behaves with a marrowbone in its mouth, you've noticed the devotion with which it shields and guards it, what care it keeps and how fervently it chews and cradles it. What moves the beast to take such pains? Nothing but a little marrow—and that seems quite enough. In imitation of this dog, I say it becomes you to be cunning in your obsessions, to smell, feel, and hold in similar estimation this ossified lot, stuffed with high conceptions, which, though seemingly difficult in the midst of their pursuit, are in the cope and carry somewhat facile...

φ

And then you must, by sedulous lecture and frequent meditation, break the bone, and suck out the marrow—which is to say the doctrines and hypotheses I target by this cockamamie mix of jibes and symbols, assured that in so doing you will at last aspire to be well-advised and heroic in their decipherment. For by the shrewd perusal of this treatise you shall acquire another kind of taste, and a system of more profound and abstruse contemplation, which will exhibit to you the most glorious sacraments and grievous mysteries, as well in what concerns your disposition in the world as matters of the public taste, and life most economical...

φ

Thus apprised of furtive quirks, of mossy fields of toxic verse, of outward brawn that covers up invisible privations; thus forewarned of swills and swells, of breathy vows and ambuscades, and every other flush and freeze of fetid exhalations, I think I shall compel us both—or all perhaps, return us all; how could I know your numbered kind, no more than your cognomen—to hold the pivot point where my concern for your uneasy truck careened so far ahead of pole position. Better the uneasy than the dead, you may reply, and with nothing but agreement from your humble guide I note that in this moment of refractory compliance forewarned is foretold, so this scrutiny is just what will direct us towards a judgment, towards an ending—our return to that malignancy most like to find the ardor of the graveyard on this hallowed ground…

φ

Such an astonishingly hypertrophic stamina, obscured by being suffixed to the subject it inclines, is distinguished from the opportune consortium of symbiotic singulars in which it participates—singularly discharged into practical extent—only insofar as that impulsion is intrinsic to its sanction as the vital, to the vital sanction it administers, and perishes in deference to its filial replacement. Is such obtuse inquiry suggested by the pertinence of the argument that precedes it? I glory in the muddle of an unthinking felicity by taking as the onus of this fluid reminiscence a decisive enterprise, where I had only meant to spell the indistinction of a trust I will not have or be had by…

φ

Still I caution not to remonstrate against the simple chaperone of this most cunning stall, the manipulative character of which is the product of its referent—of the worldly symbiosis it presumes to here recount as a description of the world—rather than its author's ingenuity. Do not, that is, allow your wit the foolish satisfactions of joining in the censure those less qualified in such pursuits consider as your one and only sensible riposte, lest your keen proprietor should forthwith seek to minimize your insults in thus barring future access to these derogating quips, and sacrifice your furtherance along this mirthful course to the god of spite…

φ

So I palpate the crude contours of my sprawling mise-en-scène, a treasure map tattooed athwart a sacrificial lamb, digging at the mark to disinter the jellied tumor from its veil of pap and sinew, from the loins or bulging occiput, or the base of the bone of the tail; every corpus is composed of such an aggregation of unwindowed individuals, regardless of the term of its debasement, or its end—by abscission, by implosion, whatever thought the genteel mode—and each becomes as nothing when extracted from the civic of its generative polis, a removal that ensures it will no longer be considered a performative vitality in prospect, or in retrograde…

φ

It's easy to imagine the slow course of its erosion, driven by the wind and rain until no lipid succulence remains to stain the pulpous fane of Gaia. Remove the respiring delictum of the tumor from its billet and it takes the form of nothing in particular, the nature of nothing else, not soft enough to burrow through with tongue or poking digit, but able to retain the distal impact of its ridges, were anyone disposed to try their hand at such caress. And should I ever yield to the allure of that engagement, I'll know to never touch the lump with naked palm or index, determined not to be *found out* by some oppressive liege or jurisdiction, and I suspect I might, were I variously inclined to the dissection of the stranger…

φ

There beside the body into which it was delivered lies the extirpated tumor just as passively degenerate as any other still inhumed within its fruiting nest; I could cut across its surface to give it some new affect, a Rosetta stone, as I imagine it—one might mount it on a knuckle to smear across the cipher, a decoder ring of some cosmetic appeal. But I am being fanciful; the recusant to the bodily ideal of life eternal—this tacit bane that I am now attempting to lay bare—is expressive of that nature by peremptory compulsion to destroy the source and sanction of its forthcoming quiescence, to pose its host as nothing more than such a patent void...

φ

What sort of adaptation is this, then, that is alone obliged to seek subversion of its maker, of its nutriment and its home? Would that it could jump from host to host like some parasitic worm, moving on when each has been sucked free of alimentary appeal, ensuring a continuance just long enough to spread its oncoseed across the mutagenic swing from drift to lineation, there would arise a new line of apes and their neoplastic keepers, racked within the thigh or lung or brainpan, the inguen or thoracic shell. I would happily receive that modal colleague as a passenger to ride within the fragile habitude my gullet would provide, to be the lonely savior of an immanence forevermore unproven, if untried by any challenge or amusement...

φ

Soothed by the entreaties of such despotic dropsy, I could finally engage in a productive form of congress and curriculum, to think myself the palatine protector of its source and supplication, succoring to plug the spaceless reaches of its ministering motherland, an otherwise unbounded and campestral stroke, as the blithe chiaroscuro of some visionary landscape spread across the sweep of tumid scree and rotted tissue. Each languorous undying must not only not die by its nature, but its reproduction also, as though to guarantee longevity from all possible directions, betraying an expansion that can only ever flourish by the equally imperative approach of its surcease…

φ

Imagine it constructed as a sort of viscous hive, its pulsing walls the rendering redaction of those minions set to occupy its structural assurance; one could slide into the trip set by one's overreaching progeny, the heart of the world—nay, of the *cosmos*—held within the muscle-gilded cage of one's own radiating mantle. There the peerless monad could take itself against itself, could build a home that as itself is of itself outside itself, to kill what it is and be what it kills, and measure off the distance from its centering intendment to the next needful alterity aroused to take its figure and its semblance…

φ

In this the succedaneum through which it first conceives itself by being other to itself indites the empty vastness of the page on which all meaning marks are blank, and everything beyond the bourne of aperture and orifice is banished from its prism of bereavements. By such belay the course of this cantankerous disposal renders its next evanescent pretense as a turn, some prototype to introduce a technology in the making, unfit for any thorough or convincing demonstration, but sufficiently suggestive to inveigle the investment of the dilettante buffoon. No identity discerned…*identified* by its discernment is ever fully realized in the employ of some periphrastic code, a trope which only cottons to contiguous coincidence as the source of its distinction—that I am, that I would be, that I ever were the consonant abstraction of the image of another, another since abstracted from an image of myself...

φ

I preen before the looking glass, adjusting my lips or combing my back or shaving my tail, whatever the ablutions required to accomplish the transparency of image unto such a witless parish of ingrates and insurgents, any dullard baptized by a gander at my aspect, as those I have encountered on my saunter past the stratum to the base. Each limpet discrepancy is stuck upon the Plimsoll line of this reposing hull, embodying the figure of the sense that is my substance—the throbbing elasticity of some first-person substrate—that I might thereby travel this precarious escarpment to the as it were...the as *I* were that's come to proof by such an ineluctable—presumably *conditional*—reasoning, to wit...

φ

Would the strained entelechy of this *vita nuova*—a fraction just as fecund as it's difficult to read—seem a most appropriate discretion, and would it have produced a teeming solitude as this unbound metastasis, surmised by its assumption into some fertile decay? How could it come to pass that so many adaptations—so many different *natures*—suffer such a pestilence, with much the same results; how, if such a dolor is construed without productive benefit—absent an advantage over those who have achieved the same by other means? Why not all expire on the order of some vicious, inborn flower, why the heart attack or stroke, the pulmonary failure or the impertinent concoctions of a viral soup...

φ

Or perchance I have the wrong approach, and it might be as plausible to conclude—in agreement with the trenchant evanescence that inscribes each bland decease—that anyone could meet an end by any means at all, as long as that's what they are forced in cusp and custom to achieve, by some corrosive tropism or adventitious churn. In this way our vicissitudes—slobbering and slovenly, shambolic and unkempt—suggest each novel speciation try and fail to reproduce some simulacrum of itself in order to ensure the next to deviate from course, only passing into novelty by breaking from compliance with the cordon of its precedents...

φ

Imagine the outrage, the loathing, the rancor and offense; imagine the merriment of merciless attackers, with their sudden jabs and bruising jolts; imagine it could possibly survive an infancy, a childhood, surrounded by those avatars of torture and suspicion, recrimination and disgust; the taunts of knavish children in the parks and fields and schoolyards, the knuckled blows and booted punts; imagine that its authors could consider it a plaything, there to live its days in the charge of brutal nursemaids, or for that much less of an expectancy in longing, writhed unto its end within some unremarkable dumpster...

φ

And be assured it won't be merely tossed from window or off rooftop; the mangled bairn will have its plumose limbs and flippers torn from silken sockets first, wings broken over ruddy knees and gills stuffed with ash till no intoxicating breath can press from out the fluid substance of the depths. Watch them prune the bowed encephalitis from its neck, to strain its lipless mouth across a savant's pitiful consent without a sound...there to speak without a sound. But I move ahead, I play my hand before all bets are in, and so I will return to where I was when...

φ

A compulsory compliance, a toil without task; be fruitful and multiply, and there among the many who engorge the unwashed province of yours and yours alone will uprear a chosen few a hair's edge off the generalized morphology of their incidental caste, to go on that same way until no other of like nature strains to execute its fitful copulation. The genus most disposed to reproduce with such abundance—most able to attain the supervenient mutation of its offspring in accordance with its practices and dudgeons—requires each within that varied membership should cease, lest none survive against the straining limits of its resources, sufficient to fulfill the pinching needs of some small portion, while the rest are left to fight over a derelict repast...

φ

No undying breed can be immured in such exigency, for there those vague requirements amount to fervid wants; thus the plaint and screed of each that *hungers* is established, who forsaken of all access to mastery and influence could never have continued even long enough to say it— to tell it as a motive or an impulse or an ending, however one delineates the consequence or cost. All else amounts to little more than whimsy, every other else desire only, but in this way the ascetic is no different from the rest; for all the hair shirts one may sport in resistance to one's yearnings, one must no less ingest and spew...imbibe and list beneath the weight of some bespoke physique, to then emit one's toxic fill...

φ

I don't know this assertion requires further proof; I hold it as a general principle, or I take it for a principle of all such treatise and pursuit, accepting every rule suggests the warrant of its predicate assignment in each instance of the set it serves to mark—every singularity within any single class of singularities, itself gainsaid by yet the same ambivalent rejection of related terms. The principle in question, if I haven't made it plain, is rather less distinct than most, more difficult to indicate by way of the indicia it ostensibly discloses, to the extent, even, that I'm tempted to resort to an *ad hominem* appeal for my proposal of a basis—of a prepossessing precinct—though even here, prostrate beneath the weight of such an undue provocation—*provoked*, that is, to seize the reigns of unrequited proof—I will have none of it...

φ

I don't know how to focus on what's always moving forward, nor how swimming towards the distance of some receding firmament can rive the drifting target of an immotile span; it makes no sense to speak this way, to cut the fallow standard of the seas with any instrument so clumsy as this tarry tail I carry, as though to paint the figure of the scapegrace with a basting brush and a vat of tar. Or rather, it is just this that makes sense—just what this speechifying takes as its first object, though the speech itself is neither here nor there...is always here and never there, or always...

φ

I have writ as much as this perverse subjunction will allow, or assemble for the lavish dispensation of the privilege; such moldered fruit, I ask—what providence deprives it of its sweetness? I know this rough-hewn trope—tropism as likely—makes not a whit of difference, and as such can't inspire any meaningful consent, but for all that it still suits me, I should say it amuses me, affirming it's accomplished by the simulated posture of this dissembled rank—the rank of interlocutor, if only to a phantom; the status of preceptor, to that departing wraith who plays the roles of pleasured rogue and sacrificial liege…

φ

I should say if I said there might be some way out of this…out of here… out of this same here this saying hereby singularly postulates, then it would come to pass and put all other baneful lasts before the tip of its unyielding consecution. So what stops me from saying it, when the saying would avoid these many obstacles to furthering the gest? What stops me from saying it? I simply cannot say. It's not that it's so easy to adopt this inclination, nor that ease or quietude could fill the empty abstract that this regress of ellipses seems to mask, all without a present to distinguish its approbative from that of any absence, of any absent absence in the distance, or the nearing next. It's more difficult to say why I have said that I should say—why I bother with this onerous performance of my own refractory languor, if not the thrilling impotence of such profane regard—when I have never had a thought of doing otherwise…

φ

It would be easy, that is to say—and no surprise at that—to insinuate a purpose only meaningfully divulged by some due diligence to come, but the privation of the effort—and the facility of the dissent—says nothing of the truth of the assertion. I am waiting, waiting for something to wait for, waiting for everything that opens up to waiting—not to be discovered, but to be discovered waiting to be discovered; I am waiting for a thought that must not be thought, that must not as it cannot, that cannot as it's always been concealed by its disclosure, neither welcomed nor excluded for having never found a trigger to occasion my deliverance from the drudgery of such coerced accord...

φ

I might beg, I might plead for an ending but one stutter step ahead of the inaugural deferral this petition has assessed, but there's nothing so appealing in these sonorous appeals, nor can they prove a balance to their own inherent suppliance—a sufficiency that designates the one certain conclusion to this emprise of reversals and regrets. My satisfaction dwells beside the point its absence points towards; waiting is an end that, by beginning in the middle...by always having since begun betrays its consummation only insofar as it does nothing of the kind—as it conceals its acquiescence from the first and through the last return...

φ

I ought to here divulge that if I here divulged an egress from this aggregate of intervals I'd surely find a method to obscure all access to it, as though by thus acknowledging the end before its advent one could skirt the view along its barren verge. I ought to do just that, I say, and yet it seems I haven't—I've said something by saying what I haven't said...by saying that I haven't said it, but saying what that saying is—what counting the uncountable amounts to, as an abstract sum—presents a problem of a different order, a survey from a vantage fixed beyond its final billet, where one's true interest lies...

V

To begin again anew, anew again, to start this time from nowhere, to begin with nothing and no one—who would want less, who would want more, as if the teller and the told were not conscripted to the coming on, the come and go, the missive grift and tally-ho, the nothing yes and nothing no, the supplement and principal, as other than, as coming to, and everything resultant; no shape, no dawn, no figured spawn, what state of grace, what world be gone, what sheer escarpment lies ahead of our trip over into...

φ

That's the trick and the catch, that's where you are, or where you should be, far from here, from every here, one wishes one could trace it, could traverse its rhymes and ridges on tracks as beaten as the day is long. It's not that I can't go there, it's not that I won't be there, but that by having been there I can't ever think to leave, and following the raillery I only just conceived in each next practice of this impotent travail against the sea, I loose the turbid rudder of my supinating tail as though it were a banderole unfurled to fill the azure apse below me, like a sail...

φ

And there is nothing for it but to wait the end, nothing but the end to come, the end where all will be the same, at last the same as before, as all that livelong day when there was nothing left to do for it, to solve for it, nothing but to gather at the terminus. Why I should begin... should have begun again in the first place or the second, or promise to commence with this indelible continuance...I have, you will agree, and so unwittingly continue, confident I've lit the furnace well for this slow burn, with chimney piercing through the breech of salivating firmaments, to hold its temperate scorch against the suppliance of clouds...

φ

The ever-waxing substance of the signatory subject, spaceless in its mass and massless in its form, is by its dreamed hypostasis displaced from the extrusion of all force that passes through it; so does reason pose as its own obviating object, and every next entelechy arisen as its rule, by which the substance of the subject—the sense of the subject as the substance of the subject—promulgates the fugitive suspension of its immanence, to-itself and of-itself and in-itself alike, the structural procedure of discernment thus administered to this the verging sense of sense, the mechanism through which every turning towards the absent bears its passenger to yet another conative cosmology...

φ

All material distinction passes through the sepulcher I'm in, the energetic quietude that shapes the thing to sense a function of the binding force exerted in the act of its receipt, and the proximal enclosure of the senses in that matrix is what unifies the substance of the subject with the tractable utility of its stance, composed alone of that sense it erects by the activity of discernment. Such constitutive confinement allows us to identify the substance of the subject sensed as the substance of the subject sensing, extended from the eye of an ape in the crow's nest to an end not the wiser in the fall from that propitiated roost…

φ

A detriment implied—stated as implied—with such an easy fluency appears to be proved true by the mere feat of allegation, but the correspondence of assertions to their transitory referents is not enough to demonstrate they are in fact or principle the case. Indifferent to fulfillment of these standards and refinements, I could as well attempt a novel discourse on the stirrings of the heart or the passions of digestion as enact a further deference to the needs of this reductive shift; I might put plough before oxen, and scratch before I itch; make of necessity virtue, and care as little for the peeled as for the shaven; sing a solemn rhapsody to simulate devotion, or signify its absence by veering from the tune—so I here declare in rough accord with my depleted lineage: never did old ape make pretty moppet…

φ

How, then, to determine what is severally intrinsic, to manifest the boundaries beyond which one identifies an empty set? The question is itself a regress in suspension, granting the particulars that illustrate this parity within its divergence—the plurality that indicates the limits of the bracket by inhabiting the class of classes, inclusive of itself—behave as though an entity convened to plot a course across its involuted surface, the pare of an interior turned out. So why leave this confusion in the path of my admirers? Why not elide the query from such indolent meander, from the tumult of this fracture, and the recoil it sparks…

φ

It's possible that's what I've done in taking this direction; how could you know, the draft of it is gone as though it never were, and no such excavation of the script as it's presented can shape the imprint of the previous upon the plumbless palimpsest of preparatory outlines and arcane fluctuations that perseveres beneath it, implied by the complexity of revisions never subsequently reckoned or evoked. If nothing else the asking of the question implies the fugue to follow—while not explicitly an answer—will fulfill my last inviolable premise, and I am nearly certain something else, having been affirmed the purpose of the access you've been granted, will have been demonstrated by it by the by...

φ

Even so I can recall another sort of promise, seeping through the cambric of this soporific pall—that I would have been...I would have been some other than...I would have been were I to seem as any other is, thereby to seize that hopeful mien as though it were the charter of some imminent inclusion. Yes, through it all I might become some fungible without exchange, without the expectation of receiving back my fill in turn, I might give myself so willfully...so *desperately* that I'd remain forevermore in that entranced possession, acquitted of the dissonance and découpage sufficiency that fortifies the fettle of all secondary modes...

φ

Somehow it all might have been if only I were as they are...as they *appear* to be from such a servile bearing, looking out upon the world from this most desolate approach, or from the dizzy isolation of some foretop spar; somehow all the sense I seem—the lickerish subsistence of this aggregate *ens entium*—does not exploit the system of engagements that most other fair to middling minds achieve by merely gazing. With a resolute proportion I'd push back into the fold, to seize a pride of place at once impulsive and unyielding; and thrust into the lead of those corralled to this occult, I'd finally accede to the forgotten, or excluded...

φ

In grandeur and in ferment, but no less in tranquil scenes, the universal fitness of the essences of things comes superadded to the surface of my unwitting attentions, the torpor of a glimpse into the latent inanition of the *noumena* presented as a closure, or a cure. Perhaps some brazen stimulant could yet propel the progress of this halting discomposure towards its harbor and its finish, so close to a babbling idiocy it's difficult to apprehend a melody or centering of themes, rather it denotes a consecration of habitual digressions, only lucid for a deference to a fragmentary cynosure, this dilating redaction of doubles and antinomies...

φ

If I could feel myself immured in such an opiating humor I might hazard an exposure to that toxic swell, but I cannot do it, I consume nothing, I produce nothing, I burn nothing somehow, someway, despite the formulary standard that trails its unction nearer to this figure of completion—*regardless of* this vulgar sheet's blank care in setting forth. I think back to the first I was as any other would...as any other world...as any other *wound*, and though I still imagine rushing full and whole into some final respite of a swoon, splitting the dead petals of that florid dust—that arid bloom—it will not do at all...

φ

It serves no purpose here for the privation…the near *absence* of all evidence in support of the assertion or any of its corollary counterpoints and claims; I don't have any sense of what I sensed before my recollection of these sullen sensitivities—I might suppose that others similarly stationed are assured their next beginning in some loose-leafed hinging of the jaw, but I am neither fashioned nor constructed in like manner, they cannot serve as models of my misbegotten form, as they struggle to comply with the intrepid correspondence I secure by my exclusion from its latency…

φ

A rigorous distinction, and quite enough for that—which in no way contravenes the place of parallel particulars within the set that fixed ideal refines. How define coherence of morphology or margin without an intimation of the given universal by which its aberrations are redacted, and opposed? If I'm to tell the difference…to *index* the distinctions of my sentience to anyone at any time at all, must not all those I task with understanding any instance of its portent be seen as equal to it, a parity that abrogates the deviance it warrants—by which I might approach the hostile terms of our engagement as the payment of some transcendental toll…

φ

In certain circumstances one can say 'As I was speaking, I thought I was saying it to you,' but this I cannot say if in any way I'm speaking *to* you at the time. So I offer you a variance…a *divergence* in the temperament I've subsequently ushered into tractate, if not open view, as the secondary inference that alleges your assent is only comprehended if it's also been deduced by each for whom it's been assembled as a posture, or a spectacle. In this sense the distinction of my kind from all the rest is centered in the absence of the intellect that chaperones my every exhalation in those who are excluded from the cordon of its membership, while asserting my ability to use that proven acumen in transit towards some practicable dissonance…

φ

Even here, even now, as I ready this archaic scrawl—and by the regulative bearing since applied to every precedent as proof—my disquisition is exceptional for being brought to bear in expectation of all possible dissension—because, that is, it must be true for any other capable of fathoming its thrust of muddled tropes and divagations, regardless of the character or force of the rebuff. I can't help but conform to what I've always been for this delinquent craving—a universal *openness* to being what I claim—understood to designate the compass of *phronesis*, an origin that's only ever realized in omission, as the inside of an empty frame…

φ

How can I regard myself the forebear of some singular similitude ascendent, conceived as though the exudate of some receding hollow at my back? How contend no other hangs above that ideal chasm, that only I can lead the fall into its sightless grasp, despite my inclination to the distance and the contrary—my drive to *carry out* the plan, my zeal only to follow? Were I to achieve the figurations I've conjoined to such comradery and kinship, to clip this caudal surrogate and reconstruct the wound I call a visage in accordance with some paragon more pleasing in its pose, staring out impassively from the implied allele of that lumpen imperium, I fear I would still manifest the foremost exaltation of this unexampled nature, if only as an exile *to myself*…

φ

Such substance can be understood a universal level only insofar as by that stamp its ends appear the posture of all reasoned intuition and imperative accord, each dislimned within the shrouding image of its perpetrating *ein-sof*—the prowling execrations of its hangman god. If I could have progressed to form some other than the selfdom I remain then that's what I'd have done, escaping through this cataract of bombast; thus I will declare myself the veiled apotheosis of what severally precedes this rotted bolster of a hull, by describing with indifference the resistance of my natured and denaturing digression from the common shear...

φ

That you might just as well avoid the plexus of this sojourn as entreat the growing distance of its dolorous distemper implies you have a knowledge of the failure of that trivial concern. I never would have recommenced but for the marvel of an epilogue beyond the rack and reach of this impoverished persistency; I *want*, that is to say, not for the purpose that first set me to the task to be mistaken for some other goal unfastened from its longing, but that what pioneered the marking of the passage should since have been completed, without the rigors of succession that would otherwise prove requisite in striking such a final pose...

φ

There are many better suited to anything but this, and all might have surveyed such a conjunction of deceits and still transfixed the seeming roundelay of this shiftless escheat; by prolixity alone I hope to eek out this quintessence of a parlor script, offered as a triumph over stasis and stagnation or a definite derangement of the chorus and the verse. I recognize that holding forth my sapience as paramount when juxtaposed with that of any comparably facultative pith presumes I have established the distinction by appealing to some intellect commensurate with those expanded faculties—by being brought along for its pursuit…

φ

Any understanding of communicable acumen necessitates that those one thinks conversant with its import be adapted to all similarly perspicacious ends, and equally the gauge by which one measures the success of one's attempts subsumes every criteria of subtlety and rectitude, either purposed with a sovereign authenticity or presented as a knowing fake. That I have not engaged exemplars of the practice—have not found a cohort equal to these acrobatic feats of phrase and fragment—has nothing to do with the fact of my assumption of that status in my throng of eager congregants, my assembly of swindlers and dolts…

φ

By this assumed sagacity I hope to further vindicate the first of any novel kind against the callow censure of some overwrought aesthetic canon—the sort that has emboldened countless litanies of dullard's prayers as literary statute and curriculum. If the fact that something lingers in its manner and its mission can distinguish its conception from all former affectations of the newfangled or fashioned, then merely noticing the repetition promises to shift it from its self-equating calm, for the sense that every instance always finds its own divergence in successive iteration towards that fascicle of supplements and termini…

φ

Each throw of the dice sequentially displays nearer coincidence with what appears the portent of the next, implicit in the wagers placed before every ensuing cast. It's a petulant assertion—a throw of the dice can never abolish chance, after all—and though I may devote myself to such prosaic poison—an instant panegyric aimed against that siren troupe—my song is always too late to correct the course; I bet the winner every time, inspiring the rage of those inclined to count themselves the cheated…

φ

An assertion need not be proved true to *be* true, a performative probity of the highest order; no leap beyond all allocutions heretofore devised to fit some affect of concupiscence—a leap I may well undertake alone—is vouchsafed by its access to such resourceful intellect, which is nonetheless exclusively distinguished by its use. If I speak only to myself it is for a cardinal purpose—that in the practice of some competence I alone possess I've found a method to traverse the uninhabited expanse by which so many of my cohort have been stymied and suppressed, struck dumb by the desperate longing…the risible revulsion that compels them to reward my gallant exploits with a treasury of violence…

φ

I might do as well to preach this to a fellowship of simpletons, and whether I'd emerge as the first among equals or would never find another shackled to the rapture to which I devote myself with each rhetorical lapse, the accomplishment still stands on its own merit— that I am, that I will be, that I have always been, an absence unappeased by any act of substitution. It's all I have, my only and most faithful lover, and I take it with a joy that few will ever know by lick or kiss or passionate embrace. Would that I could be or even *seem* as others are, then I might undergo the stasis of this program as so many have before me, to never more concatenate the ecstatic requirements of my nature...

φ

I might advise of this or that improbable disseverance, denying each its turbulence of habits and designs, a choice detail to lead my callow charges into some epiphany of vividness, it would not matter, it could not, but that in so doing I should bore even myself, and so go on, go on and on and on some other way, abstracted from the figure of that sameness, all the same. The repetition does not count...it is not *counted*, nor is it meaningful to count on such accountings regardless of the window or the view, but that I do...I do go on, I must, and so I will, it might further a digression from this digressive line, a motive that effects a first distinction from the last while still conceding to the entr'acte of some next dysmorphic trance...

φ

It's true I *have* been as I am, but that's not yet enough to specify the strata and contortions of subsistence, as though a demonstration of enduring as I was could reconcile *that* I was with *what* I was again. The question is as relevant to all similarly multiplying portents and constraints—so to think of any moment as just such a projection, or describe the path I keep to as the dreary indecision of a forthcoming retreat. Retreat from what, and fleeing into...this is not the plaint of any stray across the middle, but puts the marginalia of my varying reversals squarely on the mark you have been readied to efface...

φ

For you alone has this unruly scaffold been erected, a *menace* to diminish your return to settled ground; for you alone I drink my fill despite the bitter backwash of a vintage nearly vinegar drawn straight out of the tun; for you in having beat a lane across this patchwork chaparral, I set the scene with guarantees of public lectures, solemn resignations, the acclamations of gentle buskers and the sermons of heretical saints; I plead the case for miracles and wonders in affecting this decampment from the timeworn to the coming craze, and having had the fortitude to drag you along with me, I know you can accept the gift of insights jimmied open by your stalwart trust, your sullen gaze, and my corresponding promise to reprise the same reprisal before the next percussive blow, the next delay…

VI

Well, you may take me at my word despite salacious bearing, or defer to some mercurial criterion of rectitude in blunt repudiation of the same, but through it all I carry on in peristaltic spasms to achieve my grand assurance, and advise you in pursuance of like manner and degree—by assemblage and disturbance, extrusion and osmotic gain. Thus I will allow you some small glimpse of my compliance, what I've garnered and forsaken in the course of my pursuits; that nine parts in ten of the general use or disuse of influence in this world depend upon your motions and activities, the different tracks and rails to which you're bound and trammeled, so that once you're set a-going, whether right or wrong, 'tis not a half-penny matter—away you go a'clattering hey-go mad; and by trudging this dissembled pass over and over again, you presently make a road of it, as plain and smooth as a garden path, which, when you are fully habituated to it, neither angel nor devil shall lure you elsewise, or drive you off...

φ

I have undertaken, so you see, to write not only of my character, but my conclusions also, expecting that your knowledge of the one will give you better delectation for the other—to present some historical instruction about the biases and projections of the text and its resistances, or an intrepid catalogue of its general content together with some hesitant affirmations of the truths revealed therein. And as you proceed further with me, the slight acquaintance, which is now beginning to feel like a display of common purpose, will grow into familiarity—*commitment*, even more; and that, unless one of us is at fault, will culminate in our arrival at precisely the same start point, our convergence…

φ

But these are depths I dare not linger over; let us pivot to an instance more on level with the ordinary sympathies of the mob. Here, then, and in this remedial concurrence, we may delineate the cause of the instinct that leads—almost *requires*—the confused and the afflicted to communicate their sorrows in the form of inquisition; an unencumbered sympathy for epistolary partners whose interests are in no way concomitant with my own, and without which I would never have set out upon this philosophic junket, nor could I suppose that my narration of the *being-as* I've always been would prove an instigation to conjoin with that imperious compossible, to feel the dinkum goad of every amity to come…

φ

And what do I get by the getting there, if I've subsequently realized that I've never chanced to leave? I've said it all before—it's all been said before—which undermines the purpose of reporting on these sediments and appetites, these bulwarks and appeals. Could anyone return to that same differential supplement as readily and soon? What prescient want could justify the taking of this path a second or third time, when its maiden clamber languished at first view of the ascent? It's not as though some other mind could hope to reach a contrary conclusion with greater ease or wit, to throw its weight unto another star, or pull from that refraction the undefiled novelty of distance…

φ

In answer I accompany the outlook from the summit, a balance of position I construe *sensus communis*, but pursue as *natural law*; so all things have their end and period, and when they come to the superlative point of their transit, they are in a trice tumbled down again, as unable to abide long in that state. This is the conclusion of all who can by reason and resolve moderate their prosperities in relation to their wants and inclinations; and assuring such impenetrable surety should fail to undermine your confidence in this grimoire of a primal screech, I ask with my great master of a ribald scribe—if thy cherished house must come to ruin, why should it crush the head and clip the heels of they who in some storied past had built it…

φ

Yes, I feel the moment has arrived for me to look back, if one can understand such a convulsion as directed, or directional…to gather up my marbles on this surreptitious tilt, this littoral divergence from the shift of shiftless purchase; if only I could know what I've been saying, what I've said thus far…But no. Why bother wondering, it all comes down to one thing, always the same thing—that I am as every other ought, *alone* as every other ought, distinctly to myself as everyone must be, and as such…as such I'm the only one…the only *any* one who is both as I ought and every other ought the same. That this iterative paradox implores familiarity in all who would presume to fathom it I won't grant or deny, though as it takes the form of a disordering of faculties in those presumed its audience—and not, that is, a pose of condescension for a principle repeated as implied—it meets my stride and stratagem to do again just as I have, without extenuation. I have my faults, you will oblige, but changing my tune is not one of them…

φ

I have only to go on, as if there were something to be done, something begun, somewhere to go. That I should state this with so little difficulty, as no more than a facetious jest, there to never...to never there revisit it again...What can I tell you, where lies the fault; it calls for no small sagacity to discriminate in a narrative between the inconsistencies of its conceptions and those of life extrinsic to the rules therein set forth. Experience is the only guide here; but as all such judgment takes the form of retrospection, and thereby can't be truly coextensive with *what is*, I think it thoroughly unwise to rest one's longings and antipathies upon it. The proof is only in the doing, and I have done, I have done, as much as one could ever glean from this heroic rostrum, as a summary concern...

φ

It may appear to you I've settled nothing, that I should first revisit what I've wrestled to the fore by the pronouncement of a *given*, every proof employed to cast this breakneck swindle as a shortcut through the thicket, or a primal shore from which to sail across the mirrored sky. In this I will acknowledge we've arranged ourselves in similar suspension, and hold that recognition should sustain you in rejoinder to the claim. It could be nothing less than a fortuitous reminder; it could prove *so much more*...but I will not, I cannot, I will not do it, I must go on...

φ

On to what, you ask, and I accept the import of the question, if not entirely its answer, or the insight that its answer rests upon; what have I done thus far that I might here take shelter in some symbiotic entropy, or forevermore depart to distant shores. In order to recall adventures ceded to the farrow of an absence, a stunted shoat devoured by the sow from which it oozes, I must presume I could have been mistaken in the past, and still could have declined to understand that latency when it was most apparent…when it was *happening* both by my own initiative and through my prosecution of related acts. It's not much to admit I'm prone to error and malfeasance, but if it turns out I'm mistaken in the fix of *that* position, or any similar acceptance of a falsehood later disavowed…

φ

I can do nothing else—can assess no greater penance; I am as I will be, a guide along a pathway where no other deigns to follow, no other but the transcendental patron I presume, with full knowledge such presumption is the passage to begotten, the one way to transition from the ideal to the real. The many of the few I've known conduct their business otherwise, confusing the prosaic pace of this subdued confinement for a wallow in the slop of the sublime. Such deficit, it needs be said, can be deterred by turning one's attentions towards the insight that one's character corrals, the plenum that initiates its simpering perusals of the hoi polloi—the dulling crowd—deriving by the methods of its fluxion the remainder of what only ever pushes to delay, or go to ground…

φ

There are those who speak of justice, who portend established virtue, but by what facile bias, what banality of history, can one reside within this pose as more than a perfunctory restraint; there are those whose derogations promise some unbounded deity waits just beyond the next turn in the highway, but there's only one dominion worthy of that manic skulk, that froward shank—the dominion of ends I occupy as a sovereign gauge and channel, a ravenous explorer set to dine upon the innards of each demiurge put forward by that foremost votive quest…

φ

I might have gone the route of such peremptory perusal had I achieved this dross most high by pushing rod or pen in just below the brow, just above the vacant eye, it would only need a fragile twist to wipe the organ clean from that broad canopy of bone, that I might taste the glaucous flesh but once upon my tongue, to take hold of some sputtering ecstasis for an instant. In this I note the *grand mal* of antipathy that motivates my cohort to consider me a monstrous mistake does not sufficiently suggest some exoteric vision as my fortitude or license—as my access to the common braid, the feral caste…

φ

This is to assert more an aesthetic than a doctrine, and one might mold one's temper to compile or prevaricate in service to the caution it demands, but it doesn't serve my purpose to *describe* the disparate methods by which so many fools apply their foolishness to one thing or another. How, in the end, could such a random coalescence require one possessed of the same predicates—predicates presumed to be capricious and unique—arise coeval with it? How, when that distinction only constellates around its fractal rubric by the incidental advent of the singular? One need but once conceive the aberration to imagine its removal from the correlated field, each moment ranging farther from the agency of system, from any prescient schema, or corrosive fell…

φ

Dissembled of shape, of head, face, feet, claws, talons, beak, digits, fins, sinews; of whole parts and part parts, particles, pendicles, and appurtenances; of fragments and partitions, and all the pockmarked portions that evoke an ideal aggregate as whole hull and perfect peel, unscuffed and unpurposed; and being thus advanced in the formality of process, this deviation yields another praxis, whence arises an articulating member, that again produces a third act, fashionative of another member; which third bringing forth a fourth, procreative of another act, and so on in a like and likely manner…

φ

New members in greater number are misshaped and begotten, one still breeding and begetting another, till piece after piece, little by little, by information upon information, the process marshals all its modules; finally, having proceeded this length, and fixed this preposterous muster of lineaments into something like an aspect, one has recourse to the making of a newly fined and minted survey of these shibboleths and moorland throes, nor is it to be thought that this interruption, respite, or interpolation is herein occasioned without good reason, inducing a notable experience of a most convincing and irrefragable figure…

φ

And they could not even laugh, they could not even laugh, they could not even pity or laugh at the excretion of that palliating bilge they might have wiped from out the lozenge of a shotten pouch a vacant nest a jellied womb I could have seemed so bold I could have huffed or tried to suckle a puny sucking respirator lolling in its appetence and chiseled into stature by prehensile bough or wayward mold to idle tail fails never ordure hoof or mark above the brow and bray as though a maimed remainder greater than I was I were if only I can cull and catch and go I can and go I must I must go so I…

φ

I find it nigh impossible to stave such parataxis when the impulse hits, and keening with a bellicose insistence I expect…I *want* no sympathy for the hardship that elicited the gest, which is all well and good, given the knowledge that I'll get no more than what I've received thus far, an internecine arsenal of absences. As though such a fatality could be given as a gift—could be rescinded, even revoked; all that's given rightly—given *truly*—must be possible to renounce. It's an odd claim, I must say—I do, that is, I *have*, whether or not I must, allowing the distinction will not further be researched; I won't indulge the analogue towards which the passage tumbles, though if I did…if I *could* then this resolve would serve to fix the sweep of character I've only just found reason to reject…

φ

Someday soon one manner or another will again come to preponderate, and so I will go on—or will have done, puling my sweet prosody to any who would take me to their side, friend or foe, I could not care so long as I were acquiesced to linger in the grip of that engagement, that insipid thrall. Someday I'll be subject to a fealty of the kind…*to my kind,* that is to say, and in it…in its dissonance I'll bow before the clenching fist of thorax I imagine I commence, to happily surround the world from every outside stance, looking down upon myself as I gaze blankly skyward, and in that glare to meet with an attention I could never come to tolerate by incidental yield or charmed embrace…

φ

It would be difficult to detail…to even *notice* every marginal enticement I've occasioned by this furtive cache; the sheer proliferation of these tattered strands and partial endings makes granting any one a higher rank no more than a dissemblance of all rival paths. The advent of each dalliance in divergence seems to indicate the import of this discharge has finally come upon me, as though every dissociative misstep finds its purpose in subversion of the next. But as with any other repetition against providence, the doctrine set to bear the bale and burden of that insight only appears true if its referent has passed…

φ

To keep the hand that cuts across this capsheaf of a manuscript from landing in the midden of remembrance that surrounds it, *in limine* to brave a sea of stains afloat this sodden pinnacle of caskets, I have taken pen as sword to cut the Gordian comportment of my annals and my aspect—and I have failed, I have always failed, for having found no greater satisfaction in unraveling the tangle than this frolic in the labyrinth of its circuit. Nothing's more compelling than such focus fixed on nothing more compelling, such inference that nothing's more compelling than this…this disquisition steadied on what's excised from the outlook, from the purview and the margins, and that must surely lure some novel ends to slither forth in deed and word alike…

φ

Any egress thus discerned might be secured against all aberrant discretions…all assembled aberrations as I am, just such as I…I've done so much—so little and so much—that I might someday lift a hue and cry to something else seems an impossible demand to make of such an inert carriage. If I'd ever been invited to that bolstering of entrances, to gain habituation with another likewise fashioned—well then, I'd happily receive the assignation and seek my further fortune in the weeds, eschewing any more established brake or lineation. It's simply never happened, or if it has, I haven't recognized the boon, in each instance bewildered by a novelty of spirit fully cognate with the corpus I bestow upon the culled expanse before me...

φ

A most endearing camouflage, this blithe *Naturphilosophie*, covering the puzzlements of buttressed bricolage, and every next denial of the system it considers should construe retort within it, each polemic poised against it serving as a proof of that encountered settlement, given and dissolved. But I reveal myself too soon; or I conceal myself too late; or I move ahead too quickly—ahead of *myself*, if I haven't made it plain—in searching out the palliative bolus of encompassment, as though within the orbit of this faltering *authentis* I've found nothing to suggest any such distance...

φ

Yes, I know, or no, I mean, or maybe, I suppose...a senseless cerebration, assured that I have never...that I'll never know the difference—as though such a disquiet has stopped me in the past, has even taken my attention as far as I've allowed it to digress, but what is that to me. By the very principle this reverie would promise to unmask, the principle that hitherto administered the traffic of its pained dissemination—or *failed* in that administration, as a consonant effect—I know I can surmise the growth—at least the *clip*—and reasonably lament the decadence...the mere *collapse* of my mistakes with little or no consequence; the obverse is accounted for...is *approved* by this profession of precisely what it assays to subvert...

φ

The efflorescent ax that I have hitherto attended has now staked its feral trunk into this threshold of a coppice, and so to all who've come across this bumper of a harvest I say take what has been granted by such impious abundance, take it all, every poisoned leaf and stinking floret, make a noisome nosegay of those withered, fleshless blossoms, and then and only then think to move on. If, in the furtherance of your resistance, you feel you've been selected to play fool in this amusement, I would be the last to call your intuition wrong; it's how it would appear to me, were I the happy raconteur to stumble on this buttress, therewith to make pageant of the tumult, and the fray...

φ

And I *am* that lucky fabulist, if you don't know by now; I'm the one who flips and wheedles through this furtive peroration with a skimming eye and jaundiced glare, reduced to impassivity; who else has passed this way that they should get here first before the rest, or rest before the first...I've been here all along, that is, but this can't be surprising; I've *known* it all the while, and admitting of it now can make no difference to the victory or the loss. A rudimentary device, a childish contrivance; I have hearkened to the outside of the inside, and thought it interchangeable with any other corpse exhumed from that protruding hillock, that eternal mask...

φ

This is not meant to imply the *now* of which I speak is not an equal to the now in which I'm speaking; so many contrary contortions of the signified return the narrative composed thereby to the current of its ceaselessly protracting composition—the presence of its present, of its dilating avail—only while discerning what that consonance alleges to have finished in the preterit, but such is not the guise of this unpurposed eschaton, less inclined to entertain than to provoke in turn. One can do no better than to test one's humble merits against a summary comprised of such orphic displacements, and so accept that every nuance of the type and pagination contrives a further swim into a mortifying deference—a surrender to the parity expressed by our commitment to conjointly leaving off without requite...

φ

How strange that all the terrors, pains, and early miseries, all the binding lassitudes that interfuse the barreltone of this evasive Urizen, should ever have borne a part—and that a *needful* part—in making up the mercantile forecast of existence that is mine when I am worthy of myself. A stone flung down the wishing well that hides my near departure, I leave a trail of crumbs to trace the passage back to level, a string tied to the spur that marks the entrance to the grotto, that my erstwhile expedition might conclude where it embarked. And when at some still future now I come upon this underground and poke my reeling head in for a wink, when I find no other umbrage but the faint and dwindling profile of all possible mimesis set beneath me, I'll recognize the architect of that obtuse cosmography had sufficient pity on its occupants to offer some small hope of a retreat to the dominion of voluptuary virtue in good time, all in good time...

φ

What matter that I should feel such compassion for myself, yet for no other caught within a similar predicament? What difference if I think to drop a block or brick of marble on the tail of that lost dog, in hopes of some diversion in its recoil to panic? To service these contingencies, or in the whole indulge the involution of such crippling deceit—it takes a special skill, a certain distance and detachment, and though I wield my insight to little mean result, I do so with a vainglory no autocrat can match in terms of visionary scope or martial affect. I'm not that sort of ingénue, who thinks to shed my confines by annexing every outside; I want nothing I don't have, but the obverse isn't true—I have much that I don't want, more than it's proved possible to tally or enumerate, as any infinitum piled in the void. What's of greater worth, I ask—the savor of some sought-after contentment since achieved, or the triumphal release from one's indenture to satiety...

φ

The longing to inhabit the assemblage of an absence is equal in its way to any other want—so I slip this beaten husk as though it were a vestment, a tender seed ungird from pod, twisting off each limb to trail its pulse and pail of nerves along the bony braid of pavement. It might be I have nothing that I want, for wanting nothing—and as such I have everything I want, only more, so much more I don't believe the volume of this cosmic coffer big enough to hold it. I want nothing, I repeat, a portion always greater than the next subjunctive nullity subsumed by its concealment; if I could be possessed of that dear cipher I abjure—that has occulted my *pro forma* abdication to appearance—or place my voice within a polity of simulated masses, then every phantom index of this visionary lyric would soon enfold the silence always pressing to replace it...

φ

So I scribble on the scrawl as though there's naught left to declare, and seeking an exemption from this trailing *as-I-am*—the tenant of a syndicate whose sovereignty belies its integration with its vassal spine, its fantasy of boundlessly protracting—I set my shine and retinue against this sunny decadence of fragments. Every leech is forced to learn this verity in time—one can have too much. And as each sluggish parasite releases from its suctioned perch before it reaches surfeit, the supple thorax sloshing with the ebb and flow of every subtle swipe across its surface, I've tried to do just that in my own way and only failed, abandoned to the endless elongation of my fractured verse, my honeyed swale…

φ

I teeter and I grovel as I take in what I spew, a stinging pest whose needle is transfixed within a vascular turgidity; choked with the tumescence of a never-ending fête, I can't withdraw that feeding tube before my guts are split—whatever form such luxus takes to indicate its medium of missive. Yes, I could have been as any other is, as they are as I am… are each a superfluity I've had the lowly privilege of inscribing by the constant sway and countersway of costive ululations, a plethora that I alone am able to embolden into purpose, by indicating I alone am able to diminish…

φ

I won't belabor the point—an assertion proven false in the action of its making; it's precisely what I'll do—labor in the service of this boorish prodigality—until there's no blood left to draw from that depleted carcass. Have I accomplished anything else? I don't know; I don't care, really, but that's of no importance. If I only did as I cared to do—only followed the metrical transgressions by which I rate myself a most accomplished dancer, a most graceful shill—I'd never have begun this way, begun this parsing practicum, or crafted such attempts at its advancement. Begun, continued, ended…I have no notion what the differentiation proves, or how it could apply to anything I've done or could yet do, the invention by correction of the nothing ever different in each nothing quite the same, and in the distance…

φ

I'll always be superfluous, if nothing new or lost…if I'm *anything at all*, that is—a rendering in excess of what I thought I ought to be or could have been, always more than this *I am* I am, conscripted to the throes of such an itch in situ or anon. I've surfeited each null set feigned and fashioned in plain sight, I run each fluid figment cast out of the midpoint of this tableau of regressions, by which the vacant middle is rapaciously *filled up*; and by my lone attempts to catch a glimpse of that meridian, I've found myself positioned as its benchmark, and its charge…

φ

This is itself nearly a statement of principle, though it's surely not the principle I'll turn to proving now. There is no cause to follow lines drawn with so little delicacy, nothing to compel the exploration of each novel path that opens up a measure of declamatory rhapsody; I'd like to *interrupt*, that is, the indecision certified by such subjunctive précis, but I've wished upon that fading star before without result. Yes, I want to wander…to *move on* from this place, and as I have before…as I've *said* before, I've done so by the statement and restatement of the longing, revealing once again that there's no reason to pursue it, for being well assured of getting it—*no matter what*…

VII

Only one who is a party to the hoax can really judge, and as a party one cannot judge; hence there is no possibility of judgment in the world, only a glimmer of its promise, of its always nearing surface, nearing viewpoint, nearing level ground. But even this conjecture... this *deduction* of the principle does nothing to deter the persistency of the drive, and by implication finds every dispositive in bolstering the claim no more or less than equal to the field on which it's salted, a sophistry that substitutes the predicate of one trope for the subject of another, as though the idiom it manifests were not that of a speaker, but merely some mute rumor of a common cause. To whom that voice conducts its call...for what it has been spoken...no presently conversant drone can typify an insight set beyond this severed testament, at once our pilot fantasy of being in ensemble and the temporal luxation of a gape-mouthed *argumentum ex silentio*...

φ

If only I'd considered taking on some other purpose, perhaps a more direct approach, a second pass around the track, and having done so countless times could near the final moments of another journey to the ends of the earth—imagine what I might have been, and how I'd have revealed it. But I've done nothing of the kind; or perhaps I have done only that, I know both conclusions are somehow true and issue from the same order of premises, accepting my attempts to argue either are unlikely to seduce my addled patrons to a side. I've faced more grandiose corruptions to be sure, and I expect the thought propitiates a feeling of repugnance in those I have entrusted with this winding sheath of cringing gaffs and hobbled aspirations—those who've found release before its general flow was forced to form the recapitulation of a coda—or *preface*...

φ

For now I will petition you to pardon the discourtesy of the sentiment, and I do so with no small regret, but I won't take in another lost orphan, having thoroughly committed to the nurture of the wastrel already in my care—to thee, if it's not obvious by now, and thee alone. I've never thought myself a hero or a saint, nor a martyr in defense of my unseemly proclamations; at best I cling to the position arbitrarily and with a vulgar counterpoint, to pass off mere decree as well-reasoned syllogism; at worst I pose a fealty neither acted on nor felt, the sort that I've refused when others have adduced the disposition in considering my aspect. Of objections to my pleasure in proposing such opprobrium I offer this riposte—I am as generous with my possessions as I am eager to possess them...

φ

What reason to reveal a zealous kindness—or an obsequious antipathy—by which I might allege a mastery of artifice and disguise; what reason when there's nothing *but* this pretense to the making of the subject so derided as contingent, as randomly encountered and haphazardly devised. Having nothing, I say again, I'm munificent with everything I have. That the nothing I have is so much more than the nothing I want, or the nothing by which other outcast revelers are readied and impressed…well, we've hit upon the problem as its presently considered—as its tendered by it's adept to be tenderly dismissed…

φ

I will shoulder no more ballast than I've shouldered in the past, and for such callow penury I employ this conformation as a countenance; I'm not capable of *holding* any more than I do now, as little as that may seem—as it's been disclosed as having been disclosed—for the fullness I can barely brace my equilibrium against, as a swimmer in the riptide thinks to jump into the sky by pushing off against a wave, but succeeds only in surfacing for one last gasp. What difference if I answer the concerns of my admirers—or bow to the befuddlements with which those same degenerates are generally rebuffed; what difference when not one has lent an ear in deference or defiance, let alone proved precedent for those I've asked to join me on this secondary pass…

φ

I'll give up what I can, which is to say—*what I must*; everything that would preclude my burst into the vault had I successfully prevented its release. I don't know how to do some other than I have and still do what I do with such skilled diligence, such rigorous attention to detail, confronted with what otherwise parades as the abstraction of totality from this gathering of vestiges and scraps. I'm not making myself clear; I feel certain of it, though why I should care…I don't know why I'd care, or to whom I could conceivably direct this vague rebuke, as though I've ever known or followed rules of commutation—of common place and common parlance—understood as real by being set apart…

φ

I admit of only those bounds I'm given to transgress, pursuing nothing more than what excites the indignation of my audience of ghosts. Or perhaps that's too strong; though I may indeed exaggerate with obloquy and emphasis, it's a ploy by which I mean no disrespect. Which is precisely my conviction, my presumption, my *intent*—that while I strive to avoid insolence, I have no way of knowing if I've given that impression in any singular disclosure, nor how such knowledge might correct the course of my demurrals, allowing the prospective consolation of some imminent assent…

φ

I don't allege I've managed the success of all this pleasured speech and flimflam exposition by hearing the complaints of those among my cohort or my caste. There are none…there are none of them, as far as I can make the case, or rather, there may be none or there may be many, having recognized no method to pursue the calculation from my guaranteed position as an exile to a view of its receipt. That's the most important claim—the gist of this digression, of its intrusive reach; I have no way of knowing, of directing or detecting the affections of my comrades on this pilgrimage from flattery to disregard to subtle imprecation, even those I've gathered by this predicate decretum of a glance…

φ

An imaginary cohort is not so much made up of individuals, nor of subjects roused to manifest such individuation—in general or particular, in total or in part. They are nothing to me, I confess—each is but the equal to *every* other, which is to say no catalogue of incidental qualia will follow this remainder, applied as some collage upon…an alter always equal to the order of that thinking thinking, a thought thought yet deprived the fixed displacement of its object, but a thought thought nonetheless, or nothing more, never but that nothing more…

φ

They are only as an absence, and by no insult or indifference do I make haste in constructing these insuperable boundaries again. They are nothing to me because…well…if I must say…to admit the obvious, but still…they are nothing to me because…because *they are nothing*, they simply are not there, as far as I can tell, or if they are I don't know how to differ one from any other—one from none, by hook or by crook, by reason or encounter; I can't find a single variance between those since purported to be yesterday's arrivals and any who would spell this hapless drift across the morrow…

φ

They can't appear participants within the same enclosure; out of time, they are, though I suspect the figure of the exile from all temporal unfolding is more ably drawn by some harmonic syndicate of amiable countenance spread across its transcendental mantle, as I am most well-suited to reside within the breach. The rejoinder thus inspirited by any fitful stimulus but the flesh of the word I tell by this tell of a tail—the trailing, flaccid rudder of a wake whose jesting braille indites this requiem of lunges and reversals—is neither sacred nor profane, neither clear nor distinct, and why employ a practice or repudiate a failing if such method won't result in a discernible departure from our dispatch to the finish, our cascade to the brink…

φ

All I mean to say is that I mean to now say something else, something other than I *do* say, than I have said, than I will…And though it may prove provocation to persist with this affinity—with consistently rejecting all consistency of goal—such imperative is a reflex to precision—to *coherence*—and will repeat no matter the remonstrance of its bearer to the contrary. I conceive it as a natural right, a mythic covenant; if I appear the patsy when presented to so many better suited to the barb, at least it may protect me from their amorous advances, as they present a multitude of plucked and powdered carcasses, without character for remaining without *characterization*…

φ

Perhaps I have lost something in the bargain; the hesitations of the furtive glance, the pitying click of tongue or the quaver of a quickened pulse, the spelter tossed as some small token of a sympathetic longing, with a value only minted by that treasury of sentiment the donor thinks benighted by misfortune. I may have given up the pleasures of gentility and wit, so many fawning interviews with sages and savants, but the privation is compensated by the untold torments such absence of inquiry has spared me in response. It is a speculative gain, I am aware, but the loss is equally speculative, and I have more faith in the former than the latter…

φ

There isn't an accounting of misfortunes and deceptions that can help elude the blunders of this terminal prognosis; in the end, what I relinquish by my quizzical comportment matters little. Even this denial functions as a surplus when put against the reticent excuses and compulsive supplications that indicate the ignorance of the speaker—this accreted litany of dogmas and communions notwithstanding. Such a mastery of eristics is most readily induced by a boredom with the mannerly, accepting one need not evince that visceral withdrawal in one's commerce with the outside world...

φ

I'm confident of skipping every second in the sequence, though without a first...I'm certain the encounter only represents a pleasure by conceding an awareness of its corollary absence—the affectation of benevolence—through which I might forswear the hate more commonly performed in aid to this averred velleity, and as such I encourage every instance in oppose, each one deliquescing into some amalgamation of bone and flesh and vestment, as spring buds hanging from an arcing willow, spied from miles off. I don't know why I have so tediously eluded the enchantments of this secondary characterization—of portraying *you* in all your glorious defenses—by deducing what your vigilant attendance to the passage of this fragment makes apparent, even as I plead for a reciprocal declension in the crossing of that oceanic gorge...

φ

What could it mean, that is to say...what could it mean *to say*, when this conclusive declaration of my terms reveals I'm unaware of any patronage at any time thought present or to come, that I don't even pretend to know by whom this marketplace of distillate abductions could be fittingly attended, or systematically returned. I mean to say I say I say, and by the saying certify the practice as performed; but to whom do I say it, to what but the interstices of nebulous avidity I've pronounced the *absence* of all sentience and subject? How could I apply this censure to them all—to all I *think* they are—and yet presume the saying a superfluous indulgence, for having said already...having said as much already, or...no...I begin to confuse even myself...

φ

I have said what I have said, and having said it say no further in defense of such remarks; and if I'd settled on the impulse, I declare without remorse, I'd have remedied the trouble by excision or abstraction—in any case once and for all. It's possible I've done just that, as I've readily acknowledged, though the reminder of the always present prospect of the feint might still be salutary now. That's what's so perplexing, the sum I've never figured...what I've always failed to figure *out* by this labor of disfigurement—who it is I've *minded*, that I might once again envision the incitement to remind. Have I not made arguments to the contrary? And to whom...*for what* do I allow this inquisition to intrude upon the blackout daze its prosody elicits? To whom or what do I address this question? Who this interloper—who this quidnunc borrower—I invite to iteration by pretending to dismiss...

φ

Regardless of such narrative congruity or its absence, I'm careful to make note of every trivial deterrent encountered on my track, for the generalized belief that one can never be too rigorous in bringing the material schemata of one's triumphs and frustrations to assessment— to ostensive definition by recital or report; I know to give up poise or form or syntax—to give in to the naming of a motive or a cause— would undermine the purposes contrived by these procedures and the undeterred bewilderments they leave to our decedents on some future or indifferent course. Even so I've said too much, too much to saunter forward on this treacherous approach; I've rambled too capaciously to care...no, not that...too volubly for any interregnum to precipitate my gall or lack thereof...

φ

If I understood my prospects as divergent from all servitude, or thought I might elude the discontent of this control, then surely I would push my shriven verbiage beyond the reach of any metered ornament or dulcet thrall. Each utterance of the kind—every anomalous declamation or apportioned share—trips over the dissonance of some related query, unanswered not for emphasis or sympathy—not for the emphasis of sympathy—but for having been passed over, as the second left to slumber while the godhead reaps the life of the firstborn…Enough. I must go on to something, I must go if I have, and if I must have… if I must have then I will, as all our reportage reports that reportage reports…

φ

But the same again is *not* enough—for being always *more than*, formed in excess, as the general superfluity of any given leitmotif to its prevailing plot—and I long ago dismissed the impulse to indulge the sham abundance promised by such ill-conceived residua, let alone to think the backlog as a fable or *roman à clef*. It's not too late, I could still make that choice, even while my ongoing obsession with the sentiment proves its implications understood *before* expression. It has not stopped me yet, or it will not again, I don't know which. If I must go on perhaps I have, and might propose another similar erasure, whether I have ever done—will ever do—in the activity of defacement, soon to be remembered prior to its having been…

φ

Perhaps I have gone on—if I must; perhaps I will again—if I have; it's a safe bet I'll do something, despite…*to spite* my desire—my *need*, really—for a portion always other, always outside, always *else*; for the nothing that each otherwise must be and must have been, if I'm to soon account for this elusive satisfaction. If I'm to soon account for any such accounting, to follow through—to *make the case*—for all these failed attempts; if anything might carry us from takeoff through to landing, then it's sure to greet my notice just as soon as we prevent this lurching onslaught of remissions from impeding our attention to the slipstream, and the dross...

φ

I think I'm simply resting, the better to act when the time comes, or for no reason—to act for no reason. Better to act from stillness than from motion, but as motion seems to be our lot, I encourage you to reckon this diversion as a mode of creeping forward, of reaching for the terminus at which we're forced to part. A strange pain, the pain of crossing over, of moving *past* in lieu of steadying against, and I soon fear myself powerless to do anything ever again. It sometimes happens that we're punished for our faults by hazards and uncertainties, pleasures and inducements, in the causation of which these faults had no share, and yet I have received the most severe response to my persistence, to the error of surrender to such purposes before...

φ

The offense is of the same shape and dimensions as that which once compelled me from familiar futile glade, but the edges are jagged, and there's a dull ache that suffuses through the corpus it firstly had aggrieved. Similarly my understanding is not yet sufficiently well oiled to function short of pressure from some critical circumstance, as a violent pain one must endure without knowing its source. For there is always a consolatory feeling to suffering—an ache that recapitulates a sense of proportion between antecedents and consequents, understood by primary relation to the seed field of projected time…

φ

The sense of before and after becomes both intelligible and intellectual when, and only when, we contemplate the succession in the relations of cause and effect, which, like the two poles of a magnet, manifest the being and unity of one force by the relative opposition it manifests, and give a substratum of permanence, and therefore of reality, to the aimless mutability of subsistence. Such deliberation is not meant to incite, but to appease; not to assault, but to defend; not to conquer, but to preserve my faithful subjects and chimerical dominions in their current state—the state of infinite deferral, of resistance to discernment; the state of abdication to inertia, then redoubt…

φ

In our passion for fulfillment we will never reverse course; we make detours, we go by side roads. We see the straight highway before us, but know we cannot use it, because it's always permanently closed. The same redacted motive inscribed within another stopgap figure doesn't signify a second or third time with equal force, for all causal relation is decided by propinquity, regardless of its impacts on the chain of chance or choice. The secret is—we have only to wait, without doing anything. Without going anywhere, we will always find the shape and fill the hole the flailing burnout of our meekness and our animus leaves in payment for the damages we've wrought…

φ

And while I'll grant to those of you who've managed to stay with me through the challenges and fumbles of this second masquerade that something new may follow in the wake of its conclusion, such as I may feel obliged to render for the sake of your well wishes, while risking your attrition from some forthcoming stampede, yet I feel powerless to promise any third expedition or sally in the future, realizing the two I've already made are sufficient for the purpose of causing but a little stir, some tiny subsidence or upheaval to start things off, the whole fabric infected, spread to every venture in conception or commencement, in the middle or the end—I've set the ball a'rolling, and so doing I discharge my wont, giving good counsel to all who bear ill will to my endeavors, and expecting no divergence in the view or volubility of the same. In times of scarcity one may resort to catching songbirds, but once in hand one realizes they're worthless as a dinner fare—that they present the marrow of a voice, and nothing more...

φ

I shall remain satisfied, no less, and proud to have been the first of any scribe to have enjoyed the fruits of my work as wholly as one could desire, in absolute fulfillment of its guiding light and principles, none of which has been greater than to deliver over to the detestation of humankind the false and foolish provinces of narrative and character, even now teetering on complete collapse, and doubtless doomed to fall forevermore as soon as I've laid down my pen; still I would implore you to forgive my having carried through with all the threat and menace of this intimate remittance, searching for—or seeking out—what else, I say, but a sign of life, a ransom note, a reason to keep with you while you ready your departure, despite your heated promise that you're coming back...

φ

You know as well as anyone the bane of having given up too soon, perhaps too soon to mention—*before* you stumbled over this accretion of erasures and its auspices of ongoing mistakes, and still I carry on with such a sin against the silence that enfolds us, knowing it will come again regardless of the anger or indifference with which we further prosecute some manner of resistance or revolt. I'll continue on long after my continuance has ended, and will only cease to do so—or will only ever *have* done—when you return to find this disquisition where you left it, in the margins...

φ

And I only am escaped alone to tell thee...what? Am I words among words, or silence in the midst of silence...this is the troubling adventure that besieges our companionable egress, and has done from our meeting and arrival, no less so for myself, in noticing my words are always different, even in their repetition, but my silences—in this moment or the next, each singularly specified by reference to the nattering that surrounds it—are always indiscernibly comprised of the same predicates, and are indeed for all intents and purposes identical, no matter what or how or where the last...

φ

My silences are silent, they are plural in the singular, and singular *en masse*. The silences will come, as will the silence, it never left, but one will be aware of it...of them...that will prove the difference, from one moment to the next. Unless it's the final silence, which it always is, always this time when it's coming, never after it's progressed. If it didn't promise to end, to take the place of all that would define it by a sudden interruption of the breath, then there would only be this voice, my voice for all eternity, its mewl and howl and gasp, its convulsive clink and jangle, its litany of answers to a question never asked, and finally its proffer of a rattle and a plectrum, the frenzy of an utterance, a melody, a contraction and recovery, between beginning and ending, gaining ground, losing ground, getting lost, but somehow in the long run making headway towards a stasis that resembles a concern for truth...

φ

Such ideal reversion to the warrant of similitude—to everything that intimates its *likeness* to the real—bespeaks of an obtainable conclusion in resemblance, but that won't draw the referent any nearer to its purpose, and by further supplication to this prison of dismissals I vow only to rebalance on that figural escarpment as a salvo in surrender, or a conquest by retreat. It's not as if I might go on and then somehow I haven't, it's not as if I could continue but decide I won't; why, after all, would I think I must if I don't think I have, what reason to repeat the mantra, to chant it every time I take on something else? The quicker I do it, the quicker it will be done. Let others make their choices, the quicker the better, the nearer the end...

φ

So the waning light expires, while in the darkness that ensues we fall away into the shadows. Here and there, true to their place if not their patterns, swing sterile planets tethered to the sky, extinguished by exhaustion, or by such cunning occupants as the heat of life annoyed— who wanted to sleep in their sheds and boxes, their woods and motes and caverns, as those who would not wake again, or hitch their abdication to the banquet of the shine, no need to be far, no need to be near, without pity or scruple, fecund and barren and uncertain at the same time, to bare then spark then drive to ruin, in order to rise from the usual murmurs, in practice to dream where I am is a place, the last place, the dream of place is the last place, the final placement, and the spent world in tranquility and rancor, it isn't word, it isn't flesh, the artifice of defacers, I'll begin again, again before...

Glossary

a priori (ey pree-**awr**-ee; Latin, ā., *from* + priōrī, ablative of prior, *former*, 'from what is before') : relating to reasoning or knowledge that precedes observation experience, or proceeds from theoretical deduction rather than from inductive generalization

acclivity (*uh*-**kliv**-i-tee; Latin, ad-, *ad-* + clīvus, *slope*) : upward slope

ambuscade (**am**-b*uh*-skeyd; French *embuscade*, to ambush) : an ambush

analecta (an-*uh*-**lek-ta**; Greek *analekta* 'things gathered up') 1. a literary extract 2. a collection of philosophical musings

apotheosis (*uh*-poth-ee-**oh**-sis; Greek, from apotheoun, *to deify*) 1. the highest point of development 2. the best example of something 3. elevation to a transcendent position

argumentum ex silentio (Latin, argument from silence) : an argument from silence asserts that the absence of mentioning a field of research or a position one expects the author should have cited given an awareness of it, is explained by either said author's ignorance of it or desire to keep it from the attention of the reader

bairn (beyrn; Old English, bearn) : a child

battology (b*uh*-**tol**-*uh*-jee; Greek *battología*, stammerer) : futile or wearisome repetition in speech or writing

borborygmus (bawr-b*uh*-**rig**-m*uh*s; Greek *borborugmos*, of imitative origin) : rumbling of the stomach

catachresis (kat-*uh*-**kree**-sis; Greek katakhrēsis, *excessive use/misuse*) : the misapplication or incorrect use of a word or phrase

caudal (**kawd**-l; from Latin *cauda*, tail) 1. of, at, or near the tail or hind parts; posterior: *the caudal fin of a fish*. 2. situated beneath or on the underside; inferior 3. similar to a tail in form or function

causatum (**kawz**-at-*uh*m; Latin, effect) : something that is caused; an effect

comity (**kom**-i-tee; Latin, from *cōmis*, friendly) : an atmosphere of social harmony and courtesy towards others

consecution (kon-si-**kyoo**-sh*uh*n; Latin *cōnsecūtiō*, orderly sequence) 1. sequence or succession 2. relation of consequent to antecedent; deduction

contumely (k*uh*n-too-m*uh*-lee; Latin *contumēlia*, insolent) : contempt or harsh language arising from arrogance coruscation

decretum (dih-**kree**-t*um*; Latin, *principle, decision*) : decree, ordinance

deliquesce (del-i-**kwes**; Latin, *de-* + *liquēscere*, to melt) 1. to become liquid by absorbing moisture from the air 2. to melt away 3. to form many small divisions or branches

disembogue (dis-em-**bohg**; Latin dis- + embocar, *to put into the mouth*) : to empty, be discharged, or emerge, as water from a channel

doxa (**dok**-sa; Greek *dokein*, 'to appear, to seem, to think, to accept') : a belief or opinion, contrasted with knowledge, or *episteme*

dudgeon (**duhj**-*uh*n; unknown origin) : a feeling of offense, indignation, or anger

eidolon (ahy-**doh**-luhn; Greek *eidōlon*, from *eidos* 'form') 1. an ideal or idealized person or thing 2. a specter or apparition

ein-sof (or eyn sof; Hebrew, איןסוף non-being) : in Kabbalah, God prior to any self-manifestation. In Lurianic Kabbalah, the ein-sof must contract to make possible the conceptual space of a seemingly independent finitude

ens entium (Latin, ens *being* + *summum* highest) : In Kant, the object of the ideal of reason—an object existing only in reason itself, in contrast to the being of all beings (*ens entium*)

entr'acte (**an-trakt**; French, from *entre* between + *acte* act) : an interval between two acts of a play or opera

eristics (e-**ris**-tik; Greek *eristikos*, from *erizein, to* wrangle, quarrel) 1. the art or practice of debate or argument 2. given to often specious argument

espial (ih-**spahy**-*uh*l; Old French, from *espier*, to watch) 1. the act of observing 2. A taking notice of something 3. the fact of discovery, of being noticed

euphuism (**yoo**-fyoo-iz-uhm; after the character *Euphues*, by John Lyly, in the book of the same name, from Greek *euphuēs* well endowed by nature) : an artificial, elaborate way of writing or speaking, characterized by affected use of metaphor, alliteration, and other rhetorical props

exagmination : from *Our Exagmination Round His Factification for Incamination of Work in Progress*, a 1929 collection of critical writings on James Joyce's *Finnegans Wake*, then being published in discrete sections under the title *Work in Progress*

exordium (ig-**zawr**-dee-uhm; Latin, from *exōrdīrī*, to begin) : a beginning or introductory part, especially of a discourse, treatise, or oration

fain (**fein**; Old English, *fagen*) 1. pleased or willing under the circumstances 2. compelled by the circumstances; obliged

flexile (**flek**-sil; Latin *flexilis*, to bend) : flexible; pliant; adaptable; tractable

Forse altri canterà con miglior plettro (Italian, used by Ariosto, then Cervantes) : "Perhaps another will sing with a better plectrum"

fungible (**fuhn**-j*uh*-b*uh*l; Latin *fungibilis*) 1. interchangeable; being something (such as money or a commodity) of such a nature that one part or quantity may be replaced by another equal part 2. readily adaptable to new situations

Gaia (**gey**-uh; Greek *gaia* earth) 1. in Greek mythology, the earth personified as goddess 2. the earth in its totality considered as a self-regulating organism

gramarye (**gram**-*uh*-ree; Old French *gramaire*, grammar, book of magic) : occult learning; compendium of such

intarsia (in-**tahr**-see-uh; Italian, *intarsiare*, to inlay) : an inlaid pattern in a surface, especially in wood

integument (in-**teg**-yuh-m*uh*nt; Latin *integere*, to cover over) 1. a natural covering, as a skin, shell, or rind 2. any covering, coating, or enclosure

interregnum (in-ter-**reg**-n*uh*m; Latin, between reigns) 1. an interval of time between the close of one sovereign's reign and the accession of a successor 2. any period of freedom from the usual authority 3. any interruption in continuity

limen (**lahy**-muhn; Latin, threshold) 1. a threshold below which a stimulus is not distinguished or perceived 2. any similar threshold

locus solus (Latin, the only place) : title of a 1914 novel by Raymond Roussel

lusus naturae (**loo**-s*uh*s n*uh*-**toor**-ee; Latin, sport of nature) : a freak, mutant, or monster *mathesis universalis* (Greek/Latin, 'universal learning') : a universal mathematics or science, envisioned by Descartes, then Leibniz as foundational for all possible knowledge

Naturphilosophie (German, philosophy of nature) : the philosophy of nature developed by the German Romantics, in particular by Friedrich Wilhelm Joseph von Schelling (1775-1854)

neoplasm/neoplastic (**nee**-uh-plaz-uhm; Greek, new formation) : an abnormal growth of tissue; tumor

omphalos (**om**-fuh-luhs; Greek) 1. the umbilicus 2. the central point

ontogeny (on-**toj**-uh-nee; Greek) : the development of an individual organism or a part of an organism, or the branch of biology that concerns such development

paralipsis (par-uh-**lip**-sis; Greek *paraleipsis*, omission) : asserting something by mentioning it doesn't have to be mentioned

parataxis (par-uh-**tak**-sis; Greek, a placing side by side) : the placement of clauses or phrases one after the other without coordinating or subordinating conjunctions

paresthesia (par-uhs-**thee**-zhuh; Latin, irregular feeling) : an abnormal skin sensation, as prickling or itching, with no apparent cause

pendicle (**pen**-dik-uhl; Latin *pendere*, to weigh) 1. a subsidiary portion of an estate 2. something dependent as a subsidiary or appendage

perlustrate (**per**-*luh*-streyt; Latin *perlustratus*, wander through) 1. to inspect thoroughly; to make a thorough examination of, especially for purposes of surveillance 2. to travel through and survey (as a region)

perorate (**per**-uh-reyt ; Latin, thoroughly speak) 1. to speak at length 2. to sum up or conclude

phronesis (froh-**nee**-sis; Greek, practical wisdom) : wisdom in determining ends and the means to the achievement of them

Plimsoll mark/line (**plim**-suhl; after Samuel Plimsoll (1824-1898), British shipping reformer) : a marking on a ship's side showing the limit of legal submersion when loaded with cargo

prolegomenon (**proh**-li-gom-*uh*-non; Greek, *prolegein*, 'say beforehand') : a preliminary discussion, especially a critical essay introducing a work or topic of considerable complexity; often used in the plural **prolegomena**, even when used with a singular verb (see Kant's *Prolegomena zu einer jeden künftigen Metaphysik, die als Wissenschaft wird auftreten können*)

prolix (**proh**-liks; Latin *prōlixus*, poured forth, extended) : tediously lengthy or extended; given to speak or write at excessive length

propinquity (proh-**ping**-kwi-tee; Latin, *propinquus*, near) 1. proximity; nearness 2. kinship 3. similarity in character or nature

quidnunc (**kwid**-nuhngk; Latin *quid nunc?*, what now?) : a busybody or eavesdropper; an inquisitive gossip

reductio ad redundum (ri-**duhk**-tee-oh ad ri-**duhn**-duhm; back formation from Latin, *reductio ad absurdum*) : disproof of a proposition by showing that it leads to a redundancy

roman à clef (raw-mah na **kle**; French. *roman*, novel + à, with + *clef*, key) : a novel in which real people or events appear in fictive guise

scapegrace (**skeyp**-greys; from scape, a variant of escape + grace, someone who lacks grace) : a wayward, mischievous person

sensus communis (Latin, common sense) 1. in Aristotle, a central cognitive function that integrates and monitors the delivery of the other distinct senses 2. in Kant, the means by which aesthetic judgments are discursively—if not epistemologically—valid, by reference to commonly held standards and beliefs

shoat (shoht; Middle English, shote) : a young pig

shotten (**shot**-n; Middle English shoten, past participle *to shoot*) 1. recently spawned 2. worthless 3. dislocated

sublunary (suhb-**loo**-nuh-ree; Latin, beneath the moon) : mundane, earthly

succedaneum (suhk-si-**dey**-nee-*uh*m; New Latin, substituted) : a substitute, especially for a treatment or medicine

thews (thyoos; Old English, custom, habit) 1. muscle, sinew 2. muscular strength

tumid (**too**-mid; Latin, *tumēre*, to swell) 1. swollen; distended 2. protuberant 3. pompous; bombastic

Urizen (**ur**-*uh-zuh*n) : in Blake's mythology, one of the Four Zoas, the fourfold division of the central deity, embodying conventional reason and law

vox et praeterea nihil (Latin) : voice and nothing else

Steven Seidenberg's works include *Anon* (Omnidawn, 2022), *plain sight* (Roof Books, 2020), *Situ* (Black Sun Lit, 2018), and *Itch* (RAW ArT Press, 2014). His books have been published in Italian, Portuguese, and Swedish translation, and his photographs have been published as *The Architecture of Silence: Abandoned Lives of the Italian South* (Contrasto, 2023) and *Pipevalve: Berlin* (Lodima Press, 2017).

Coda
by Steven Seidenberg

Cover art and design by Steven Seidenberg
Cover typeface: Bauhaus 93

Interior design by Laura Joakimson
Interior typeface: Garamond Premier Pro

Printed in the United States
by Books International, Dulles, Virginia
Acid Free Archival Quality Recycled Paper

Publication of this book was made possible in part by gifts from
Katherine & John Gravendyk in honor of Hillary Gravendyk,
Francesca Bell, Mary Mackey, and The New Place Fund

Omnidawn Publishing Oakland, California
Staff and Volunteers, Fall 2025
Rusty Morrison & Laura Joakimson, co-publishers
Elizabeth Aeschliman, production editor
Sophia Carr, production editor
Rob Hendricks, poetry & fiction editor
Jeffrey Kingman, copy editor
Sharon Zetter, poetry editor & book designer
Anthony Cody, poetry editor
Liza Flum, poetry editor
Jennifer Metsker, marketing assistant
Avantika Chitturi, marketing assistant
Angela Liu, marketing assistant